BO

THE JAPANESE LONG STAFF

DESIGN/Danilo J. Silverio

DISCLAIMER

Please note that the publisher of this instructional book is **NOT RESPONSIBLE** in any manner whatsoever for any injury which may occur by reading and/or following the instructions herein.

It is essential that before following any of the activities, physical or otherwise, herein described, the reader or readers should first consult his or her physician for advice on whether or not the reader or readers should embark on the physical activity described herein. Since the physical activities described herein may be too sophisticated in nature, it is **essential that a physician be consulted**.

Unique Publications
4201 Vanowen Place
Burbank, CA 91505

ISBN: 0-86568-082-5

Published 1986. Printed in the United States of America.

ABOUT THE AUTHOR

Tadashi Yamashita was born in Japan in 1942. However, he considers himself an Okinawan. His father died when Yamashita was three and his mother, who never remarried (the older Japanese did not believe in remarriage), moved her family to Okinawa in 1950. He lived in Okinawa until 1964, when he came to the United States for good. He is now a United States citizen.

Yamashita, who has more than 27 years of experience in the martial arts, began his study at the age of 11. The roughest kid in school, Tadashi not only picked fights with other students, but also with his teachers. This was brought to the attention of the school's parent-teacher organization, which realized no one could handle him.

One day, the PTA president, who also was a karate instructor, stopped by to pick up Tadashi after school. Always the warrior, Tadashi even tried to fight him. The instructor slapped the rebellious youngster and dragged him off to the dojo where he was taught the elements of kicking, punching, and most important, discipline.

Tadashi found his probationary period very interesting. His destructiveness was channeled into his hidden talent. The young man had discovered an art form, a religion, a way of life. Yamashita was 16 when he received his black belt. In 1960 he captured the all-Okinawan Shorin-Ryu Free Sparring Grand Champion title.

Tadashi has been a versatile athlete. On Okinawa, in addition to mastering the martial arts, he was also an outstanding baseball pitcher. He also has collected more than 60 trophies for his prowess in motorcycle racing.

When he came to the United States, he owned and operated a karate school for five years. In 1968, Tadashi went back to Japan and became the youngest seventh-degree black belt in the country's history. Among those judging his performance were his instructor, Sensei Sugura Nakazato, a ninth-degree black belt, and grandmaster Chosin Chibana, a tenth-degree black belt.

In 1972, in search of a fuller life, Tadashi moved to Southern California, where famed karate practitioner Mike Stone was among the first to recognize his awesome karate and weapons talent. The Pro-Am Tournament in Los Angeles in 1973 was the first of many opportunities for Tadashi to display his talents. Some 7,000 fans gave Tadashi a standing ovation at that tournament after watching one of his demonstrations. And from that moment, the magic of his karate-weapons genius spread throughout the martial arts world.

During the same year, Yamashita was featured on the television show, "Thrillseekers," with Chuck Connors. Mail poured in from all over the world hailing Yamashita's prowess. After his appearance, he was signed by Tohe Productions and later starred in his first motion picture, *The Karate*. Tohe also used Yamashita in two more films, *The Blind Karate Man* and *Karate II*.

Some of the American films in which Tadashi has appeared are: *Enter the Dragon, Judge Dee, Golden Needles,* and *Octagon* with Chuck Norris. Other film credits include: *The Seven, The Magnificent Three* and *The Shinobi*. His television credits include many appearances on "Kung Fu" and "A Man Called Sloan."

Considered the foremost karate and weapons expert in the United States, Yamashita is the head instructor of the American Karate Association, as well as the head instructor of shorin-ryu karate in the United States.

TABLE OF CONTENTS

HISTORY OF THE BO

In the 14th century, Emperor Hashi ruled Japan. To halt possible foreign relations with China, he gathered his troops, including many battle-hardened samurai, and invaded a small island called *Ryu Kyu*. Later, that island became known as Okinawa, a small parcel of land in the Pacific Ocean, which measured 16 miles wide and was inhabited by thousands of farmers.

Once Hashi took control, his first order to the Okinawan citizens was to surrender all weapons. Despite this edict, fighting continued as the Okinawan citizens battled to maintain control of their country and themselves. To say Hashi's soldiers were ruthless would be an understatement. They were cold-blooded killers who would take whatever they wanted from whomever they wanted. They would let no one stand in their way.

While this attitude benefitted the Japanese in the short run, it turned a once-peaceful Okinawan people into a vengeful mass bent on securing its release from the dastardly clutches of Hashi's henchmen. Clearly, they were a people with a cause; the fire of freedom raged unchecked in their hearts.

However, there was a major problem. No war has ever been fought, or more importantly won, without weapons. And Hashi had taken care of that by confiscating all weapons when he assumed control of the island. The Okinawan people, though, were considered an industrious lot. What they lacked in numbers and modern technology they more than made up for in raw grit and determination. Consequently, they used whatever they could to protect their families and property.

Because farming was such an important part of the Okinawan lifestyle, Emperor Hashi allowed the people to keep their farm implements. Since they were considered harmless tools, Hashi had no reason to suspect the Okinawan people would use them for anything other than beating rice, digging holes or carrying water. The Okinawan people, however, thought differently and soon realized seemingly harmless farm implements could be transformed into weapons of deadly force.

By utilizing different pieces of farm equipment—generally with certain modifications—a new crop of weapons sprung up to take their place in martial arts history. Although there are many theories, it is believed a simple tool used to carry pots of water may have helped drive Hashi and his samurai from Okinawa. Carrying water from one place to another was too difficult for smaller Okinawans. So they used a piece of wood from nine-to-12 feet in length to help balance the load. By placing the wooden pole on their shoulders, and then tying the bags or pots of water to each end, the load was balanced and easier to carry.

However, when combined with martial art movements, the long stick or *bo* suddenly became a vicious weapon of self-defense.

The Okinawan people had long been known for their skill in the empty-hand martial art of karate. The fluid movements and tremendous power were famous throughout the Orient. However, against the sophisticated—for that time—weapons of the samurai, their empty-hand moves were ineffective. But when those same forms were joined with weapons, the Okinawan people immediately became a force with which to be reckoned. The Okinawans grew in strength and power but kept the newfound art a secret—until one night when the samurai soldiers of Emperor Hashi discovered just how deadly the combination could be. One evening while some of Emperor Hashi's samurai were getting drunk on the beach, the townspeople gathered their new weapons and attacked the unsuspecting samurai. Not one Japanese soldier was alive when the dust settled. The Okinawan people had made a very strong point.

Stunned and embarrassed, Emperor Hashi couldn't understand how a people without weapons could massacre anyone, let alone his prized samurai, considered by many to be the finest fighting machines of the time.

Eventually, word spread of the battle, and of the prowess of the bo and other farm-implements-turned-weapons of destruction. The lessons learned on a beach one summer evening were passed through succeeding generations. Only through the use of these tools could the Okinawan people stave further attacks from outsiders.

Further developments resulted in the bo being used for sport entertainment and as a means of passing time.

When I came to the United States in 1964, I introduced the bo in demonstrations by placing an apple in the mouth of one of my students and then smashing it out by using the weapon at full force. Immediately, the weapon became popular with other martial artists.

However the bo is used today, whether for sport or recreation, its place in Okinawan history cannot be forgotten. Once a simple and harmless aid for carrying water, the bo grew to become one of the most important weapons in Okinawa's arsenal of self-defense. Necessity, it is said, is the mother of invention. In the 14th century, the people of Okinawa needed a weapon to stop the tyranny and oppression of a ruthless Japanese emperor. The invention was the bo.

Great Okinawan Masters

No book about the bo would be complete without at least a small mention of some of the famous Okinawan masters who placed the long staff among other great martial arts weapons. Among the great many bojutsu practitioners of Okinawan history, we take time to honor four:

Sakugawa—He was one of the country's great karate and bo experts. Born around 270 years ago, Sakugawa was sent to China by the king of Okinawa on a fact-finding mission. Enticed by some of the Chinese martial arts, Sakugawa spent approximately 10 years learning the Chinese arts in addition to perfecting his bo and karate styles.

Tsuken—Tsuken lived more than 300 years ago, but it certainly was not a happy life. An expert in karate as well as the use of the bo and sai, Tsuken accidentally killed someone and became the target of an angry samurai bent on revenge. Once caught, Tsuken was bound and tossed in the ocean to drown. However, the great warrior freed himself and found refuge on a nearby deserted island, where he hid during the day and trained at night. When he finally returned to Okinawa, he was hailed as one of the country's top bo practitioners.

Soeishi—He was assigned the task of teaching a deaf-mute who was the son of the king's bodyguard. Famous in the 1600s as both a karate and bo master, Soeishi worked long and hard to train the boy. One day, the youngster dropped his bo and heard it hit the ground. From then on, Soeishi was regarded as an Okinawan legend.

Gino Wan Donchi—He spent a great deal of time as Soeishi's servant. And during that time he was able to peek in on his master's workout. Soon, he picked up his master's forms. One day, Soeishi walked in on his servant and was surprised at his proficiency. He then agreed to take on Donchi as his student.

WHAT IS THE BO?

Listen to some martial artists and you'll likely hear misinformation about the bo. According to some people who call themselves experts, the Okinawan bo (the name was shortened from roku-shaku bo) must be a cylindrical piece of wood from six-to-12 feet in length. Also, those same experts claim there are only several variations on the bo.

This is not true. Simply, the bo can be any thin piece of wood used for self-defense, exercise or recreational purposes. That means a walking stick is a bo. So is an umbrella or two-by-four. The same can be said for a baseball bat, broomstick or mop handle.

The traditional Okinawan bo measured between nine and 12 feet in length and was used by low-ranking farmers and fisherman either to carry water or other items. Later, martial artists cut the length of the bo and created the jo stick, which measured four feet in length, or the hanbo, which was three feet long. The modifications were made because the length of the bo did not allow for easy concealment. The decrease in length permitted people to hide the stick under their long flowing clothes.

Okinawans in the 14th century, however, did not just pick up a stick off the ground and immediately call it a bo (although in a pinch the makeshift weapon would have probably been effective in the hands of a trained practitioner).

The original bo or Japanese long staff was made from oak, considered one of the hardest and least-destructible woods available. Once the tool was cut and measured, Okinawans placed the bo over an open fire to rid the wood of any moisture. This prevented rotting and made the drier wood unbendable. Once the moisture was removed, the practitioner then laced the bo with one or more coats of oil, usually whale or pig oil (however, any animal oil could do the job). The oil not only gave the tool a fine, shiny finish, but also helped strengthen the weapon. This time-consuming ritual caused traditional bo to turn black in color. Today, however, bo come in an array of shades.

Most traditional practitioners also kept the bo in an upright position when it was not in use. This not only kept the tool from warping because of the moisture-laden Okinawan air, but also prevented it from being stepped on or damaged in some other manner.

The bo was one of many farm implements the Okinawans used as weapons of self-defense. Others included the *nunte*, a bowlike spear that was perfect for spearing fish in the shallow marshes; the *tonfa*, a one-and-one-half foot long wooden stick originally used for grinding grain; the three-sectional staff and its cousin, the double stick or *nunchaku*, both of which were used to beat rice or other grains.

Theoretically, the bo should be three inches longer than your height. So, if you're six feet tall, you would want a bo that measures at least six feet, three inches, or 75 inches.

An easier way to tell whether or not your bo is too short or too long is to place a hand on your head and extend the thumb and forefinger as wide as possible. Your bo should be as long as your body plus the extension.

The reason for the extra length is one of protection. You want your weapon to be long enough to reach your target without placing your arm or hand within striking distance of your attacker. The optimum bo could strike at will and still keep the attacker a safe distance away. Thus, the bo was very effective in old Okinawa against the weapons of the samurai.

BOJUTSU: LEARNING TO USE THE BO

The long staff may be simple to find and make, but the path to mastering the art of bojutsu is anything but easy. Although I was introduced to the bo when I initially took up karate at the age of 11, I was not allowed to practice the weapon for two years.

Most karate *sensei* maintain it takes two years for a practitioner to learn karate basics. Only after a student has had a healthy indoctrination into the martial arts is he able to grasp the innerworkings of the bo or any other traditional weapon.

When my instructor in Okinawa handed me my first bo, it was not for the purpose of practicing weapon techniques. We first had to carry water with the bo, just like our ancestors, to learn that the center or middle is the focal point. Only by remaining in the center, only by remaining balanced, can the nuances of karate be appreciated and utilized.

In Okinawa, once you have a foundation in karate, instructors will let you have any weapon. But getting to that point is very difficult. A practitioner must learn the meaning of focus, balance, coordination, speed, power, distance and timing. You just can't give anyone a bo and expect him to know what he is doing; they don't know how to focus and the weapon will be worthless. But put the bo in the hands of a trained practitioner and watch the weapon sing. The weapon becomes an extension of the karateka's hand. A block in karate is much more effective when the bo is introduced. A karate strike takes on a new meaning when the bo makes impact.

Like most weapons, the bo has myriad uses: striking, parrying, tripping, arm locking, spearing, poking, throwing and fending. A particular use will depend on a specific situation. For instance, when confronted with a knife-wielding attacker, you could use the bo first to fend and then to cut under the legs, strike at the knees, poke in the chest or strike at the head.

In any case, the practitioner should always be concerned with the middle. This is where leverage comes into play. This practice is different from those who study the Chinese bo. Because the Chinese never used their body to carry water in the manner of Okinawans, they hold their bo at the end.

In accordance with the study of karate, aikido, kendo or jujitsu, learning bojutsu means mastering the 13 movements associated with the Japanese martial art. Those movements or patterns are karate's foundation.

When used correctly, the bo will resemble the motion of a windmill. The practitioner will always be twirling the weapon, always trying to keep the attacker from having a clear area in which to aim. You are forever protecting the middle. Two of the more popular patterns in bojutsu are the *windmill* and the *jug of water*. In the windmill, the student places his hands about two inches apart at the center of the bo and works the weapon in fast-moving, figure-eight motions. The movements should confuse any attacker, since he will not be able to find an opening. The jug of water pattern comes from the way old Okinawans held their hands when they carried water. To maintain better balance, the hands are placed about two feet apart at the middle section of the bo.

In all cases, the uninitiated should not use this book as the sole training guide in their bo study. Proper training in karate basics is a must to mastering the bo. The bo can be dangerous when handled by someone who is not familiar with its properties.

BO EXERCISES

No matter how skilled you are with the bo, failure to properly exercise will drastically affect your performance and may lead to injury. These exercises are not difficult, but they are highly effective. And they only take a few minutes before practice.

Strengthening the wrists

1. Both men face each other while holding the bo in the middle.
2. The man on the left pulls the bo, while the other provides resistance.
3. The same procedure, only this time the man on the left provides the resistance.

Strengthening the shoulder muscles

1. One man holds the bo behind his back, his hands at shoulder width. The other grabs the bo inside his partner's grip.
2. While the man on the right is pushing up, the man on the left is trying to pull down.
3. As the man on the right is pulling down, the man on the left is pushing up.

Arm exercises

1. Hold the bo in front with a tight grip, hands about one foot apart.
2. Lift the bo over your head. Make sure your arms are straight.
3. Pull the bo down hard.

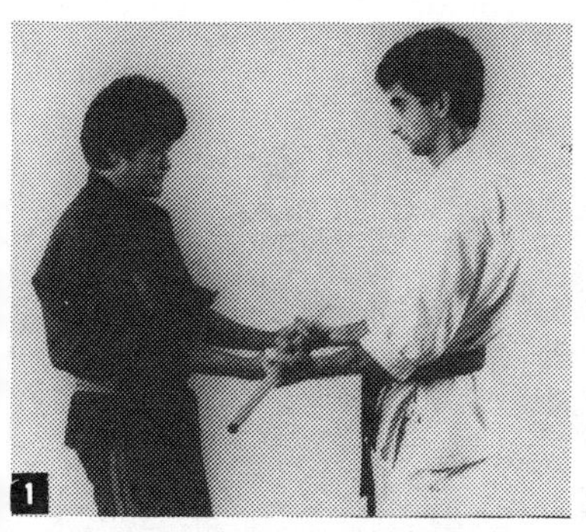
1

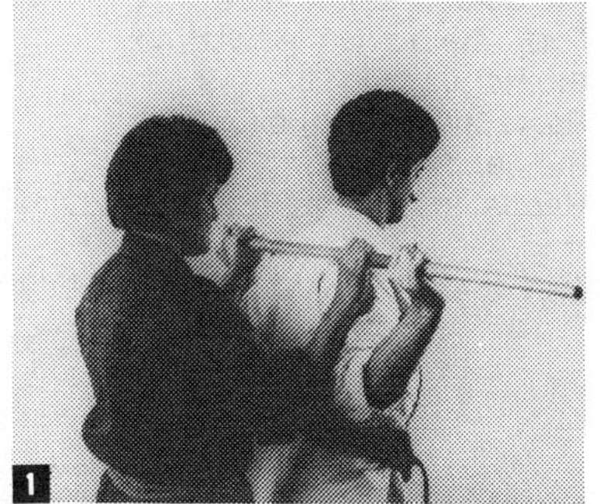
1

1

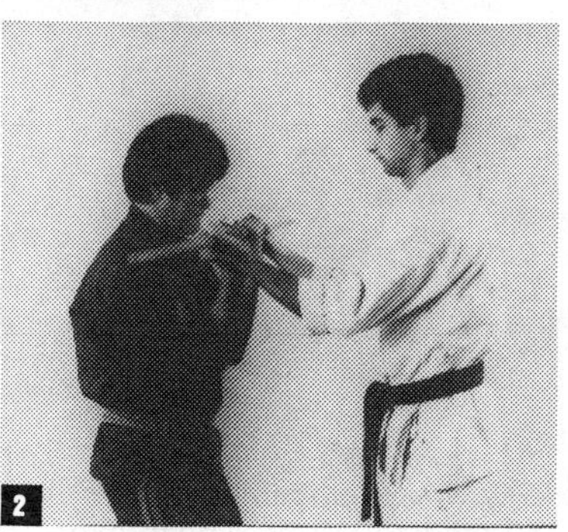
2

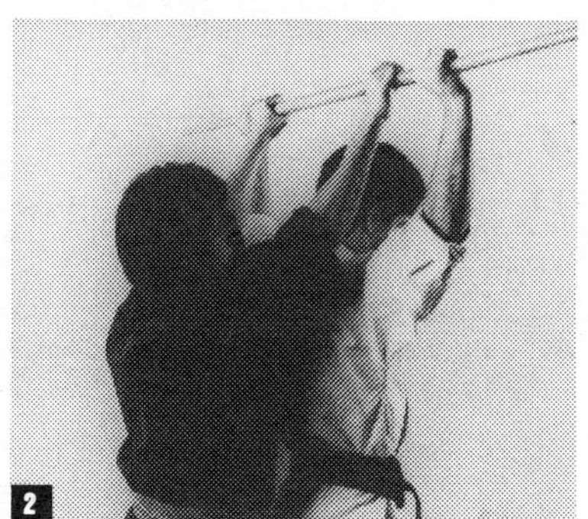
2

2

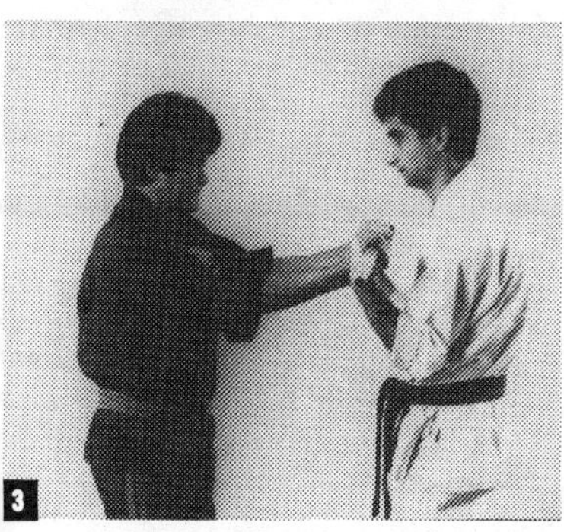
3

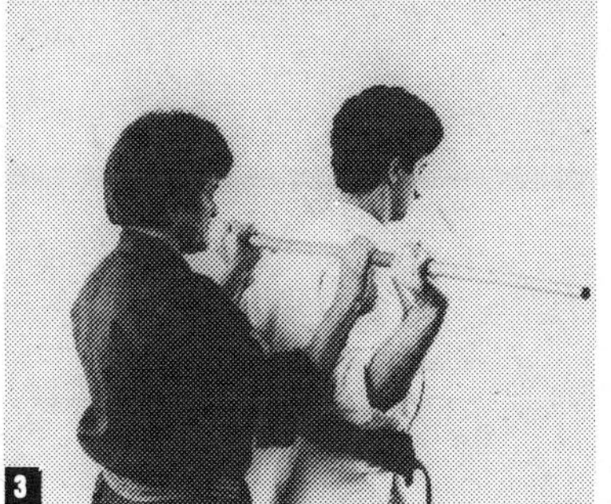
3

3

◄

1. Bo should be perpendicular to the chest. The left hand is over and the right hand under the end.
2. Squeeze the bo and twist down hard.
3. Squeeze the bo and twist up hard.
4. Squeeze the bo and twist down hard.

►

1. Assume a forward stance, with both hands holding the bo across the face.
2. Drop the bo, while twisting the hands.
3. Raise the bo, while twisting the hands.
4. Repeat step number two.

1. Start in a horse stance, with the bo straight out and the hands positioned right over left.
2. Lift bo over head.
3. Pull bo down.

1. In this two-person exercise, each practitioner should hold the bo at the neck area.
2. Pull down simultaneously.
3. Push up simultaneously.

1. Each person grabs an end of the bo.
2. Squeeze and twist the bo before pushing down.
3. Bring the bo back up while twisting and squeezing.

1

1

1

2

2

2

3

3

3

◀

1. Start in a set position, with the right hand holding the bo, your elbow cocked and your weight on your right foot.
2. Thrust forward and place weight on front foot.
3. Spring back into original position.
4. Repeat step number two.

Coordination exercises (figure eights)

1. Start with bo in an upright position.
2. Move the right wrist down and the bo tip will follow.
3. Turn the wrist up and the bo tip toward the sky.
4. Turn the wrist over so the closed fist shows the fingers facing outward.
5. Bring the bo all the way down.
6. Turn the wrist over again.
7. Return to the original position.

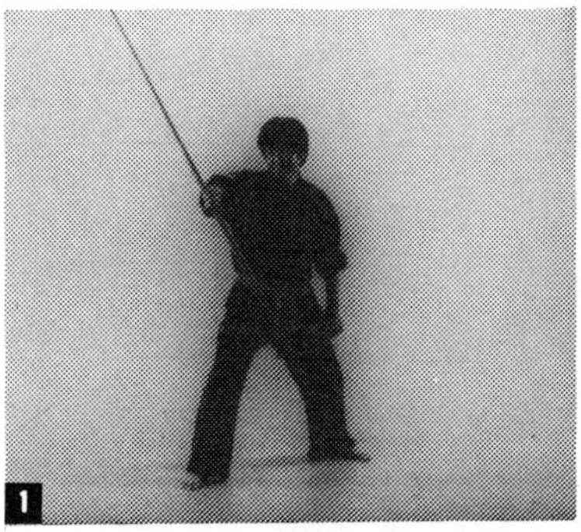

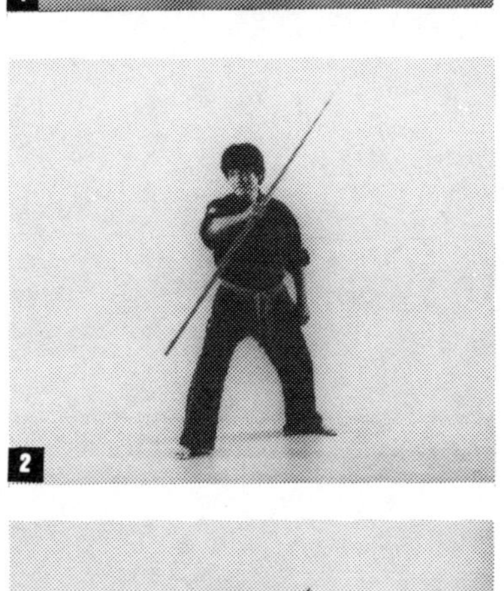

2

5

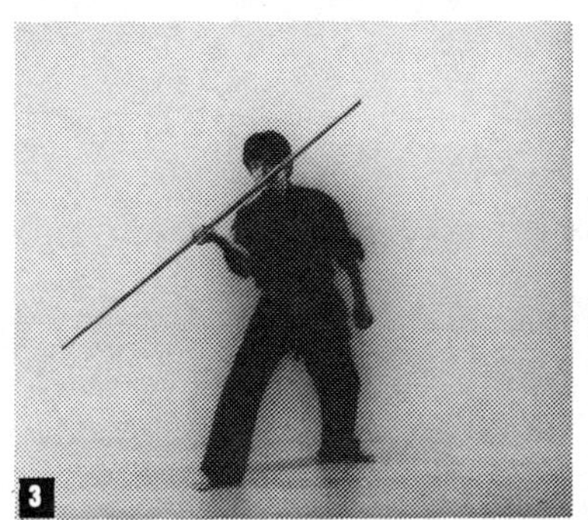

3

6

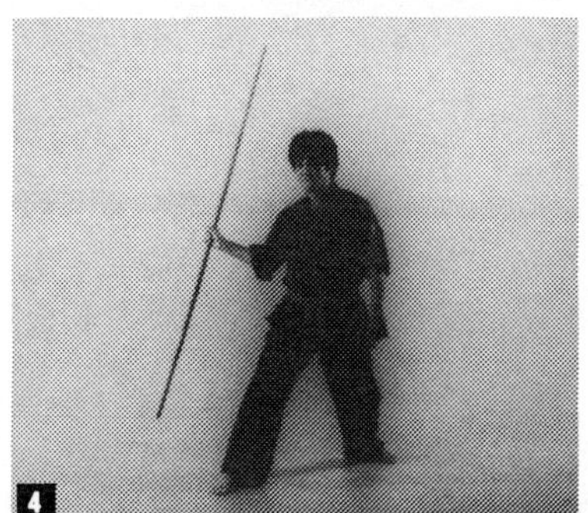

4

7

1. Start with the bo horizontal, and your right hand over the center of the weapon.
2. Turn the bo and your wrist into a vertical position next to your body.
3. Spin the bo across the back of your wrist.
4. Catch the bo with your open right hand and return to your original position.
5. Start again.

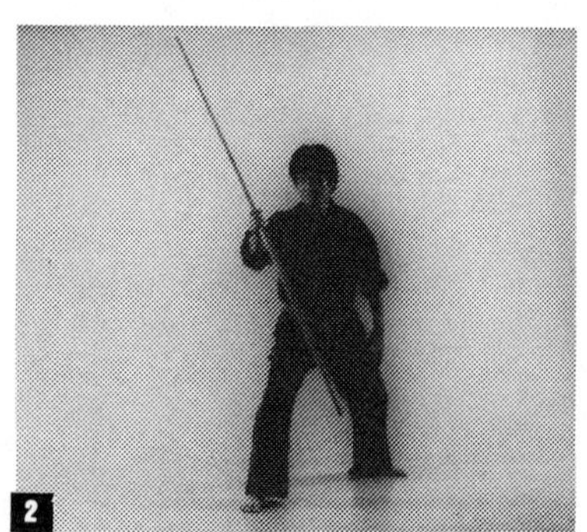

1. Start with the bo in a horizontal position at chest level.
2. Twist the bo and pull it vertical to your side.
3. Twist the bo quickly with a flick of the wrist.
4. Release the bo, letting it roll over your wrist.
5. Catch the bo with the open hand.
6. Return to your original position.

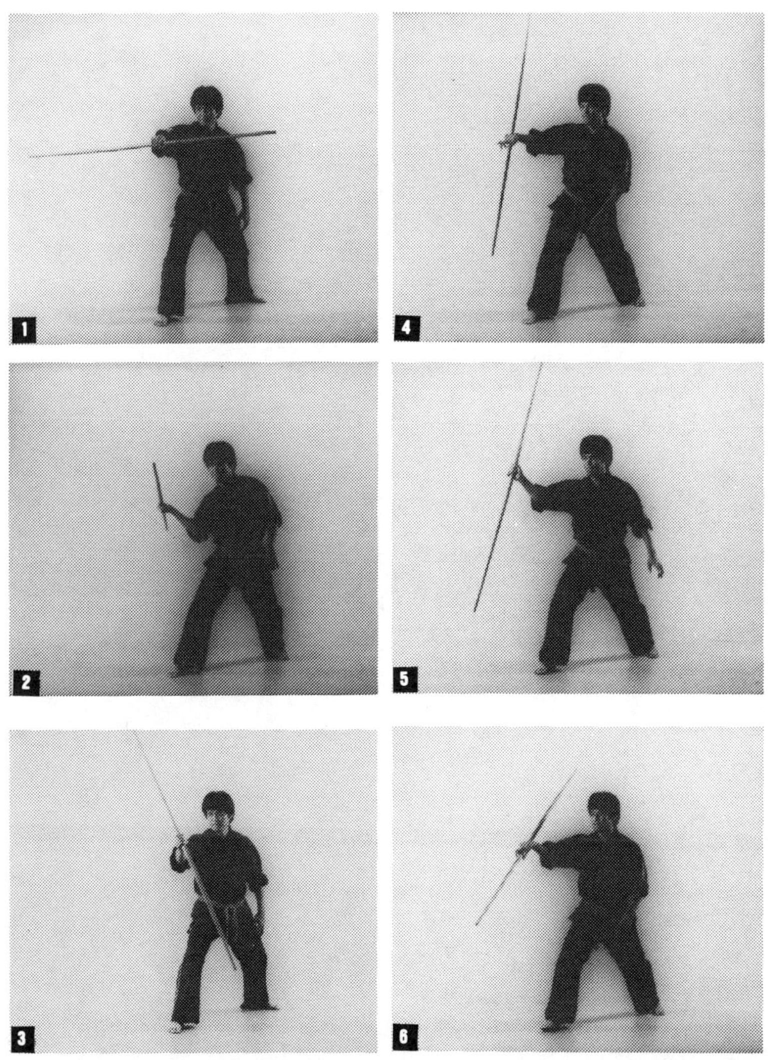

1. Start with the bo in a vertical position.
2. Drop the top of the bo toward the floor. Your hand should be above your head.
3. Push the bo behind your back from right to left .
4. Grab the bo with your left hand.
5. Flip the bo and return it to its original position.

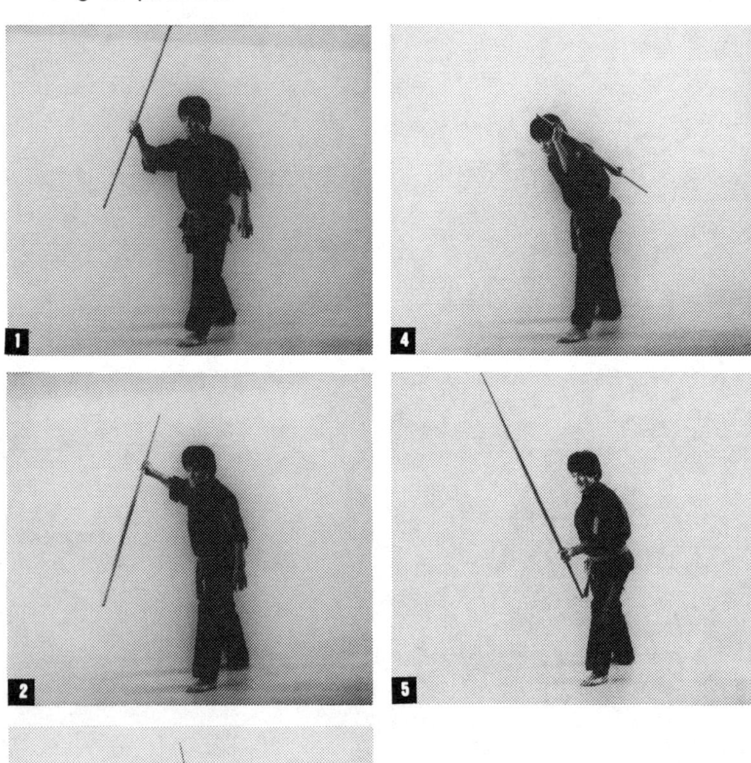

▼

1. Start with the bo at a 45-degree angle. Your hand should be toward the top.
2. Bring bo across your chest and spin your wrist. Release the bo.
3. Let the bo roll over the top of the wrist.
4. Catch it with your open hand.
5. Return to your original position.

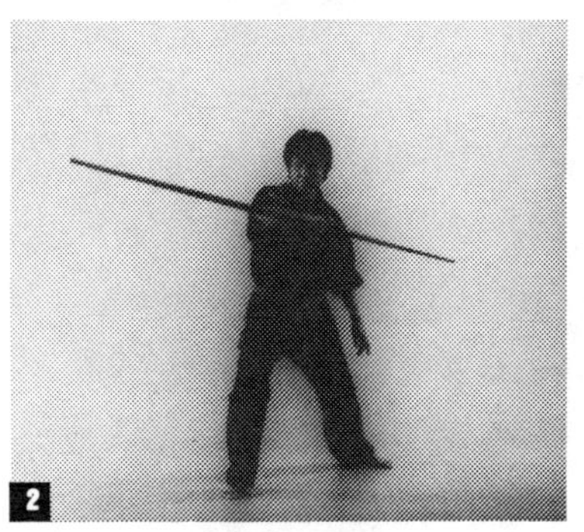

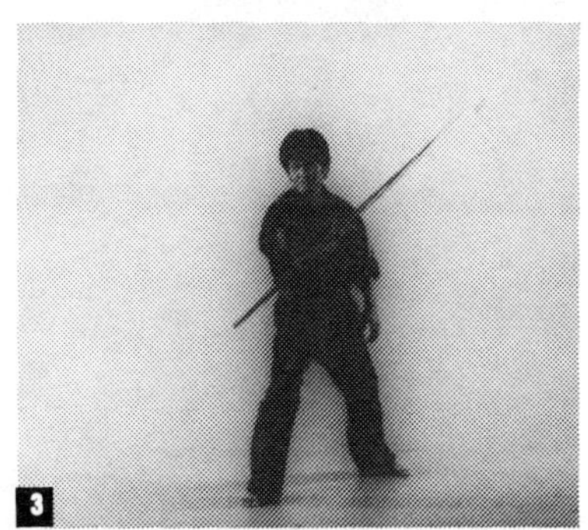

►

1. Start with the bo diagonal to the floor.
2. Bring the bo across your body and over to your left shoulder.
3. Take the bo with your left hand.
4. Swing the bo across your body in a snapping motion.

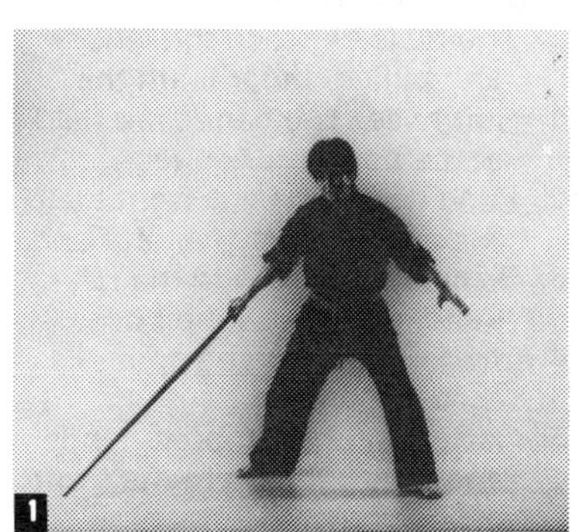

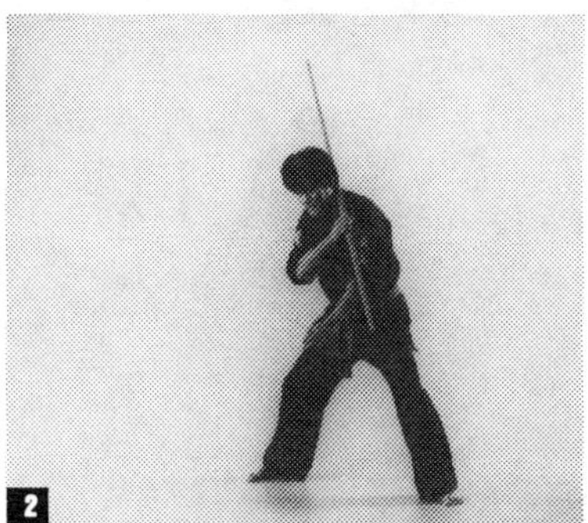

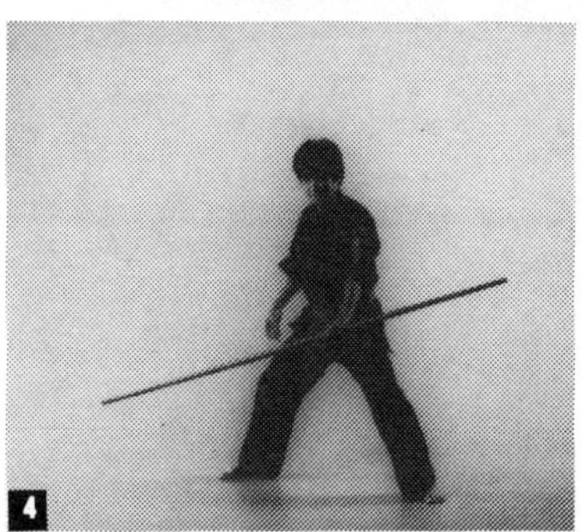

Hand exercises

1. The bo is between the legs and pulled underneath the left knee. The hands are held at the bo's outer edges.
2. Push down with the right hand and pull up with the left hand.
3. Bring up the bo with the left hand and across the body.
4. Let go of the bo and spin it across the wrist.
5. Catch the bo with both hands and return the bo to the front of the body.

1

4

2

5

3

1. Start with the bo behind your back, your hands underneath and close together.
2. Pull out the bo with your right hand and hold vertical.
3. With a circular motion, sweep bo across your body.
4. Grab the bo on top with your left hand.
5. Twist wrist and turn the bo over.
6. Drop the bottom end of the bo behind your back.
7. Grab the bo with your right hand.
8. Pull out the bo with your right hand.
9. Twist the wrist and hold the bo at an angle.

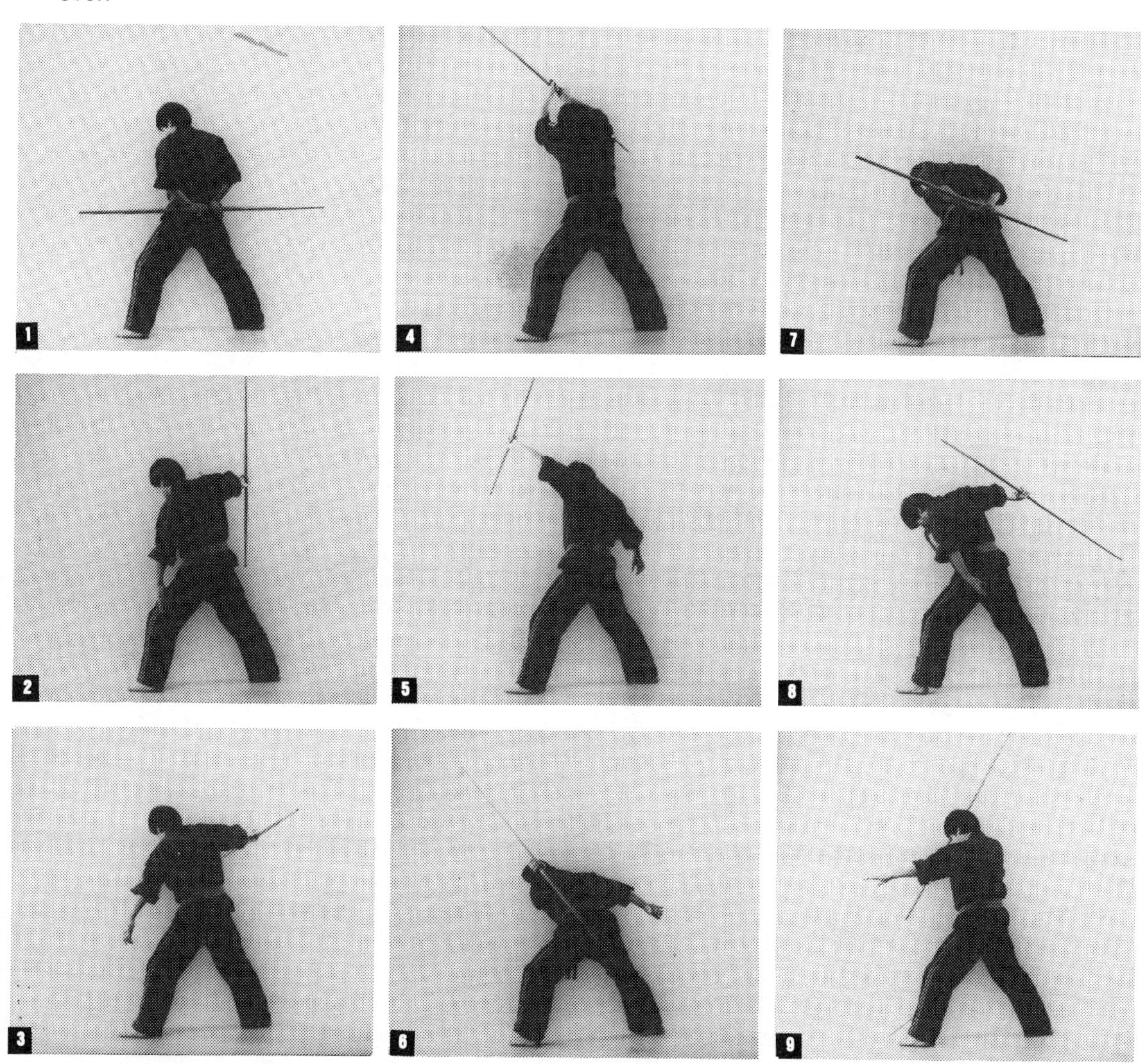

1. Draw bo, as though drawing a sword.
2. Bring bo all the way back.
3. Put bo back, as though placing it in a scabbard.

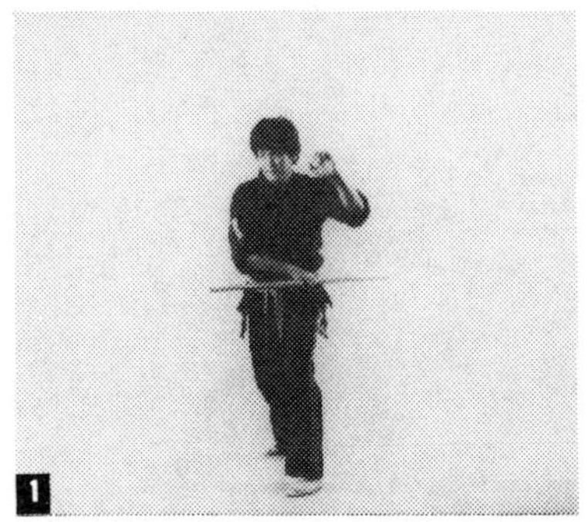

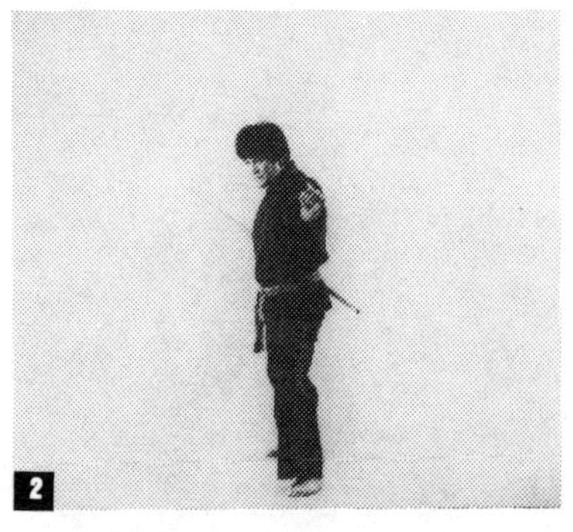

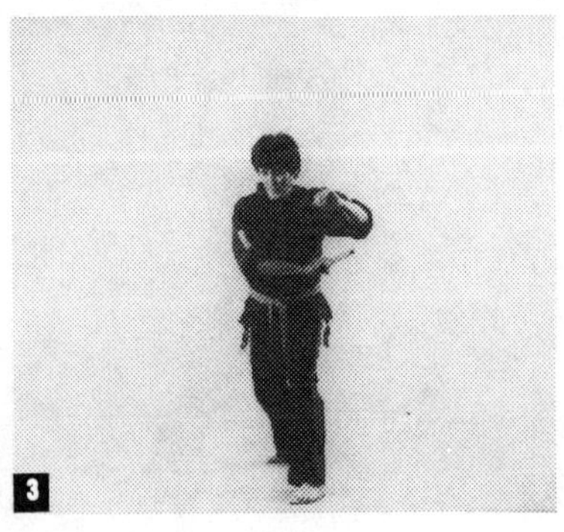

1. Hold bo, with the left hand over and the right hand under.
2. Pull out, twisting right hand over left.
3. Let bo slide as hands change position.
4. Now the left hand is under and the right hand is over.
5. Repeat the movement and return to original hand position.

▼

1. Start in ready position.
2. Bring the bo down and across your body.
3. As the bo comes across your body, twist your wrist. The bo is vertical.
4. Pull the bo back up.
5. Twist the wrist down and the bo will follow.
6. Return the bo to the front of your body.

➤

1. Hold the bo in front.
2. Bring the bo across your body and over your shoulder.
3. Let the bo roll over your shoulders.
4. Catch the bo with your left hand.

1

1

4

2

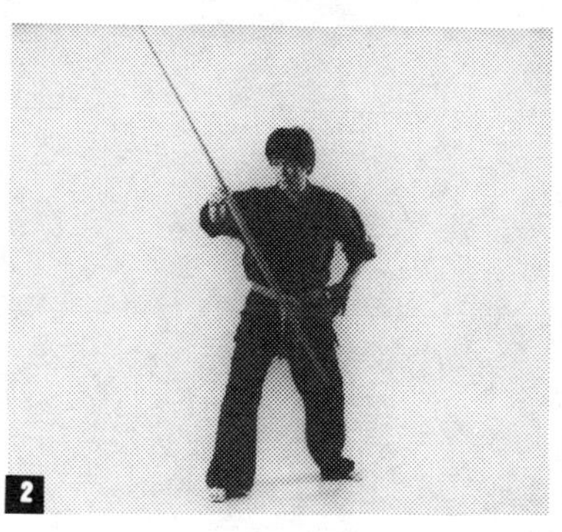
2

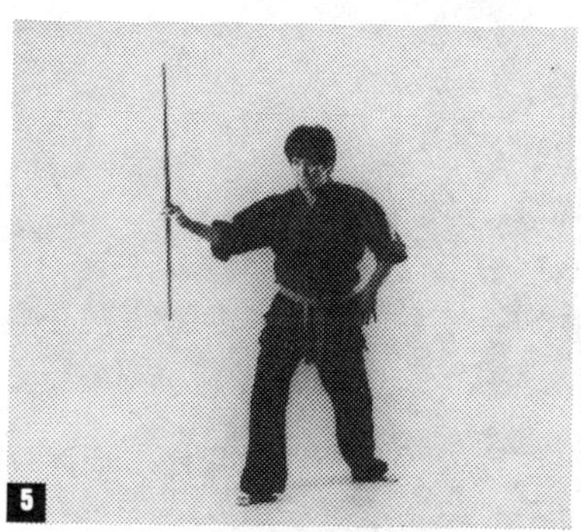
5

3

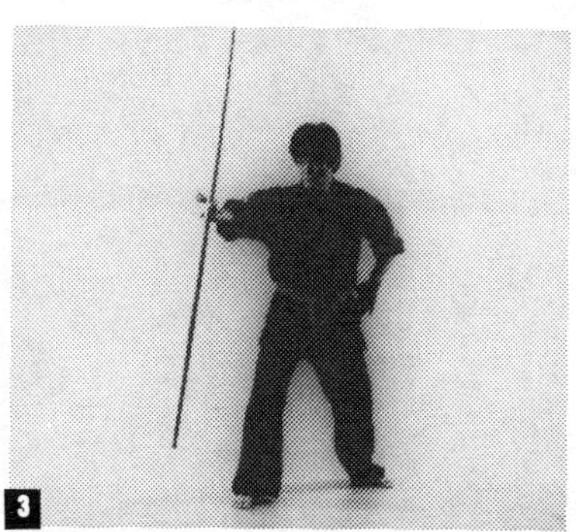
3

6

4

THE STANCES OF BOJUTSU

Although there are no definite stances in the ancient Okinawan martial arts, the most useful and effective positions against an attack come from the stances featured in karate training.

The stances shown in this book are essential to bo techniques. They must be mastered because the accuracy and instantaneous power needed in karate depend on stance training.

Your stance must be stable enough to create a block in the event of a strike, but also flexible to allow for quick reaction and changes during an attack. Without the stability of a stance, your opponent's strike may either hurt you or throw you off balance. Without the flexibility, you will not be able to adequately adjust to changing tactics. The ancient Okinawan martial arts sometimes require the weapon to be free to move independently of the body. The stance, then, must allow complete harmonious movement in any situation.

The three kata I present are the suna kake no kun, or the basic flipping sand technique, the choun no kun, or morning cloud, which was always practiced at dawn, and tsuken no kun.

With any kata, you must remember: know your kata backward and forward; be conscious of your breathing; keep your body focused, yet loose, and stable yet flexible.

BO KATA

Suna Kake No Kun

1. Start in ready position with hands forward.
2. While in cat stance, turn left and lift bo.
3. Drop bo, as though ready to flick sand.
4. Flick bo toward sky.
5. Lift left leg and flick back of bo.
6. Drop left leg.
7. Snap and strike with front of bo.
8. Turn 180 degrees and thrust forward.
9. Drop bo to the ground and assume cat stance.

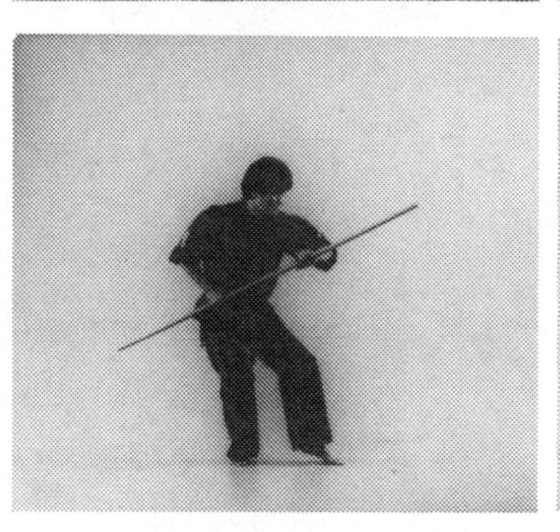

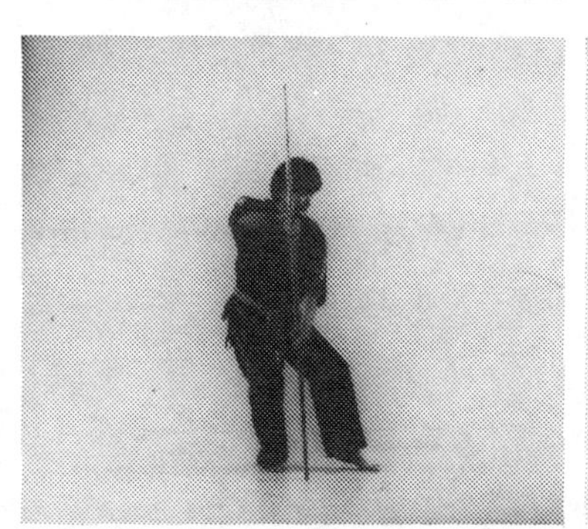

10. Flick bo toward sky.
11. Lift right leg.
12. Twist bo and thrust forward.

13. Twist 90 degrees to the right. Bring bo vertical.
14. Lift right leg and twist bo to horizontal position.
15. Pull bo toward your chest.

16. Strike by snapping left hand on bo.
17. Turn 180 degrees to right into *kamae* position.
18. Lift left leg and twist bo horizontally.

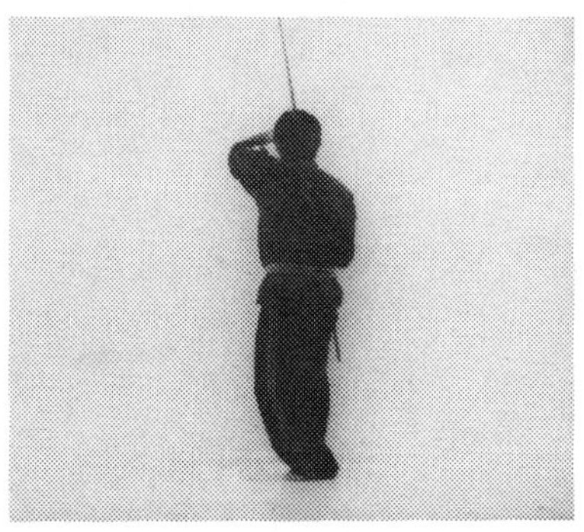

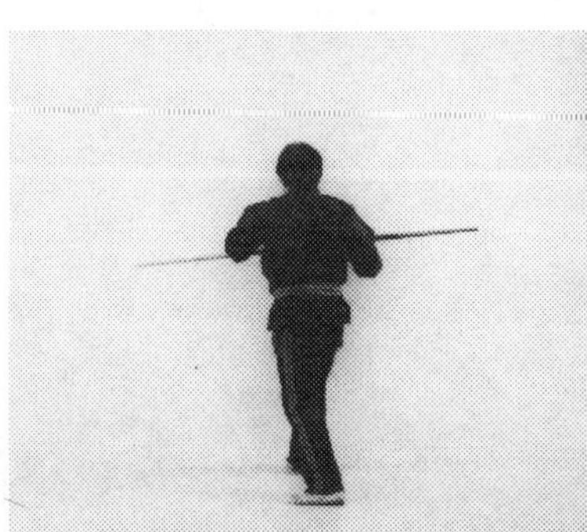

19. Pull bo toward chest.
20. Snap bo with left hand and strike with butt of bo.
21. Drop bo tip to the ground.

22. Flick up bo.
23. Pull bo toward chest.
24. Use right hand to snap bo.

25. Drop tip to ground.
26. Flick up bo.
27. Raise right leg and pull back bo.

28. Step forward with right half-moon strike.
29. Bring bo to left side of body.
30. Use a crossleg movement and prepare to strike.
31. Thrust bo forward.
32. Turn 180 degrees counterclockwise and pull pole vertical.
33. Lift left leg and pull bo horizontal.
34. Step forward and thrust.
35. Drop bo to ground.
36. Flick as though throwing sand.

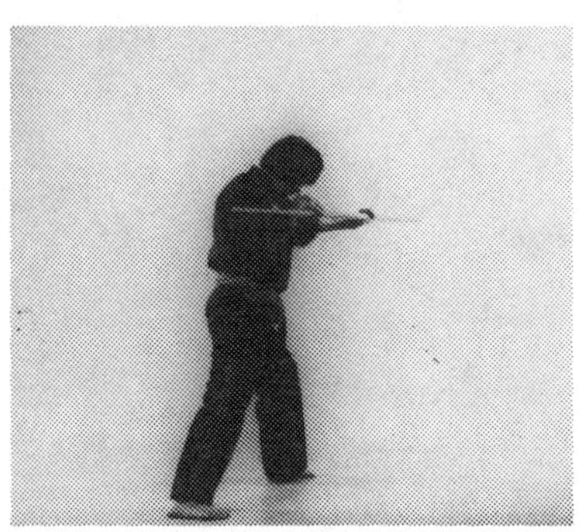

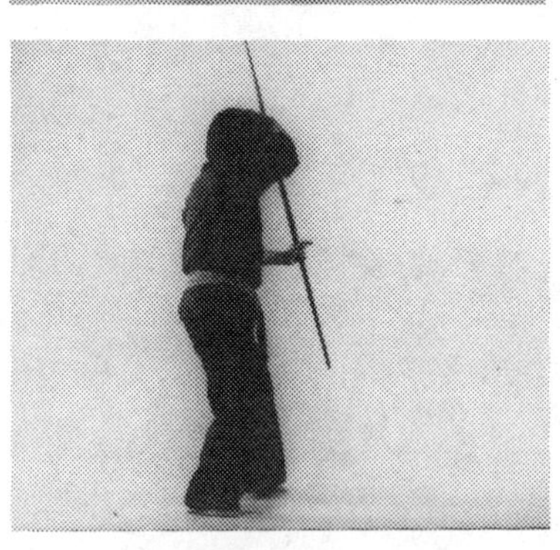
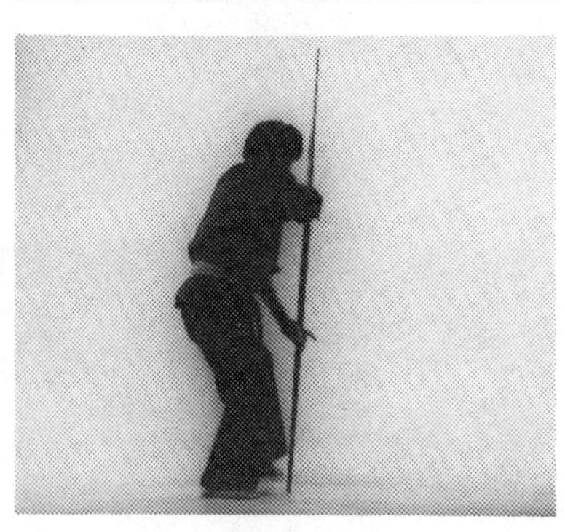

37. Step forward with right-hand strike.
38. Drop bo to ground while in cat stance.
39. Flick up bo.
40. Lift right leg and bring bo toward right side.
41. Drop foot and prepare to strike.
42. Step forward and follow with right-hand strike.
43. Step to the left 180 degrees counterclockwise.
44. Raise right leg and bring bo toward chest.
45. Step forward and follow with left-hand strike.

46. Step forward with right leg.
47. Prepare to strike.
48. Follow with right-hand strike.
49. Right leg returns to normal position.
50. Lift bo toward sky.
51. Drop bo to waist.
52. Finish in normal stance.

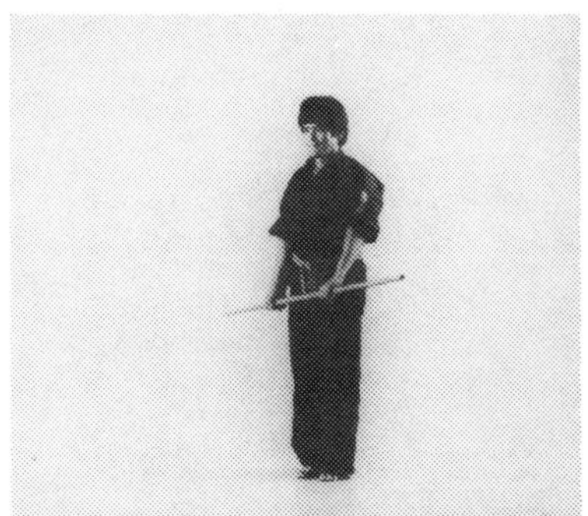

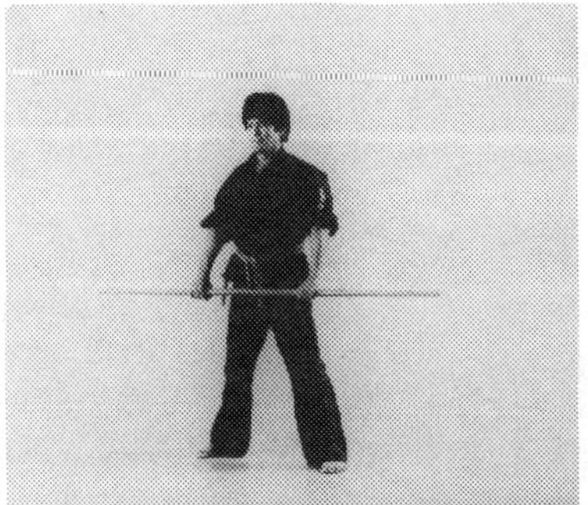

Choun No Kun

1. Stand in ready position, bo at side.
2. Turn left, reach back and grab bo with left hand.
3. Step with right foot and swing bo downward.
4. Finish with bo on right side.
5. Swing the bo to the left side.
6. Assume cat stance and block.
7. Step forward and strike.
8. Step back into cat stance.
9. Step forward.

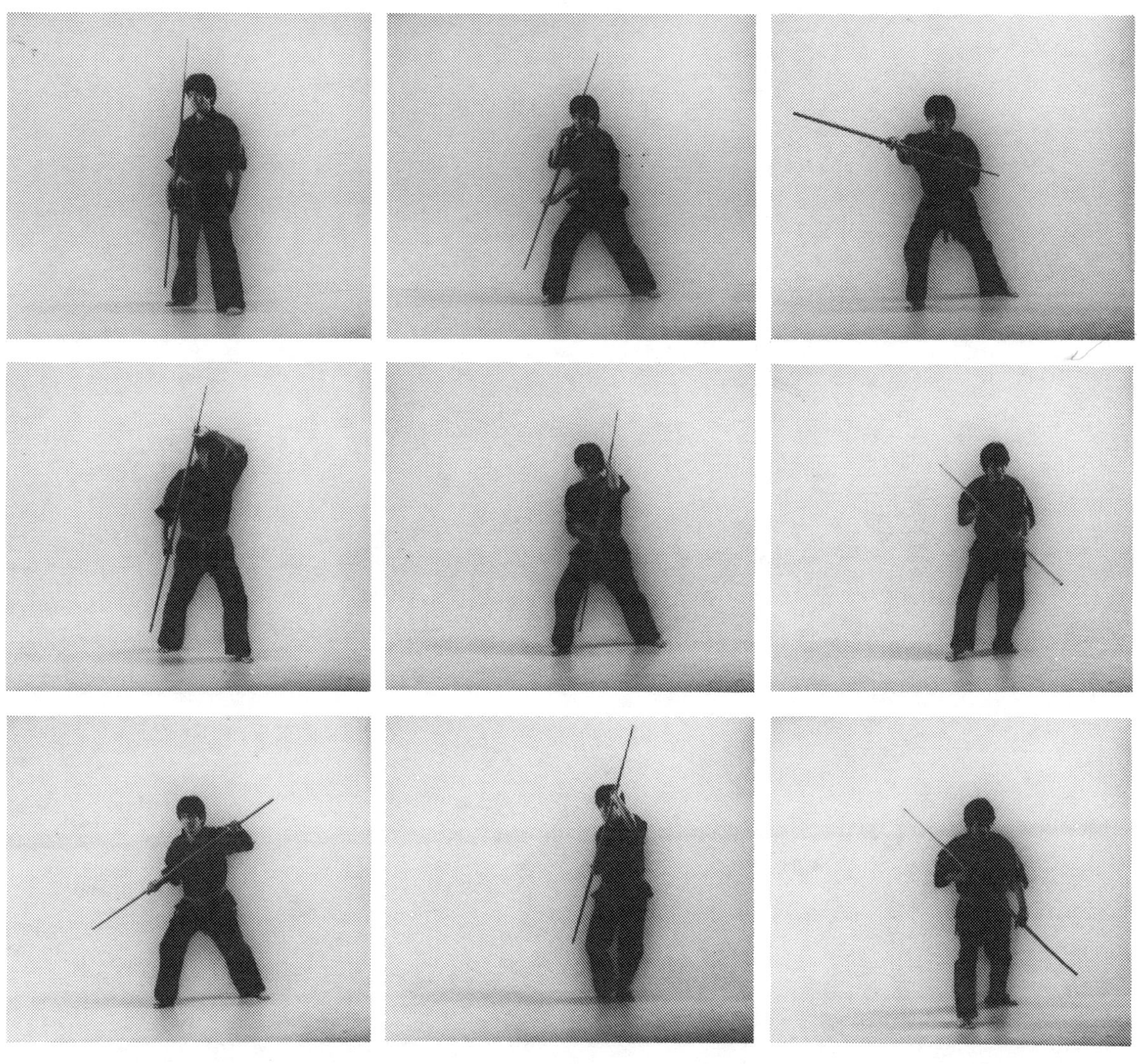

10. Apply a downward strike.
11. Step back into a cat stance.
12. Prepare for a middle block.
13. Step forward and turn up tip.
14. Prepare for a downward block.
15. Lift up the tip.
16. Hold it over your head.
17. Follow with a downward strike.
18. Pull the bo back.

19. Assume a strike position.
20. Follow with a right-hand strike.
21. Change hands so left is on top of bo.
22. Step forward and prepare to strike.
23. Follow with a left-hand strike.
24. Prepare for a right-hand strike.
25. Step forward with right foot.
26. Follow with a right-hand strike.
27. Pull bo back and drop into a horse stance.

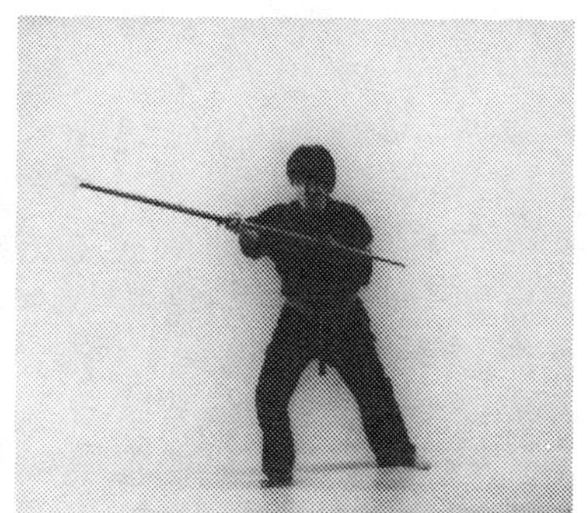

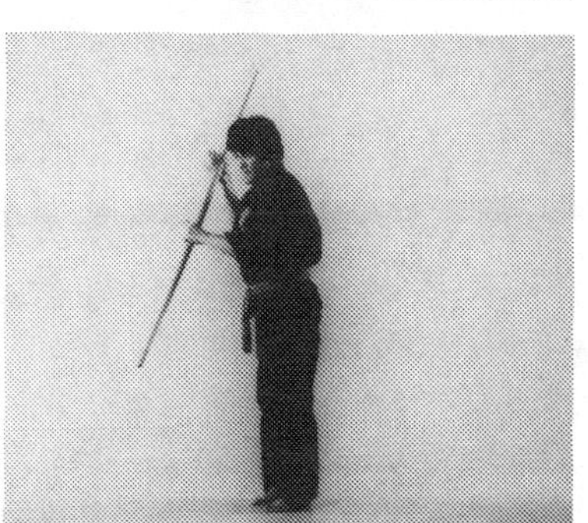

28. Left hand drops into a low block.
29. Low block position.
30. Raise left leg.
31. Turn 45 degrees counterclockwise.
32. Prepare to strike.
33. Follow with right-hand strike.
34. Kneel on left knee and pull bo back.
35. Prepare for an upper block.
36. Follow with a right-hand strike.

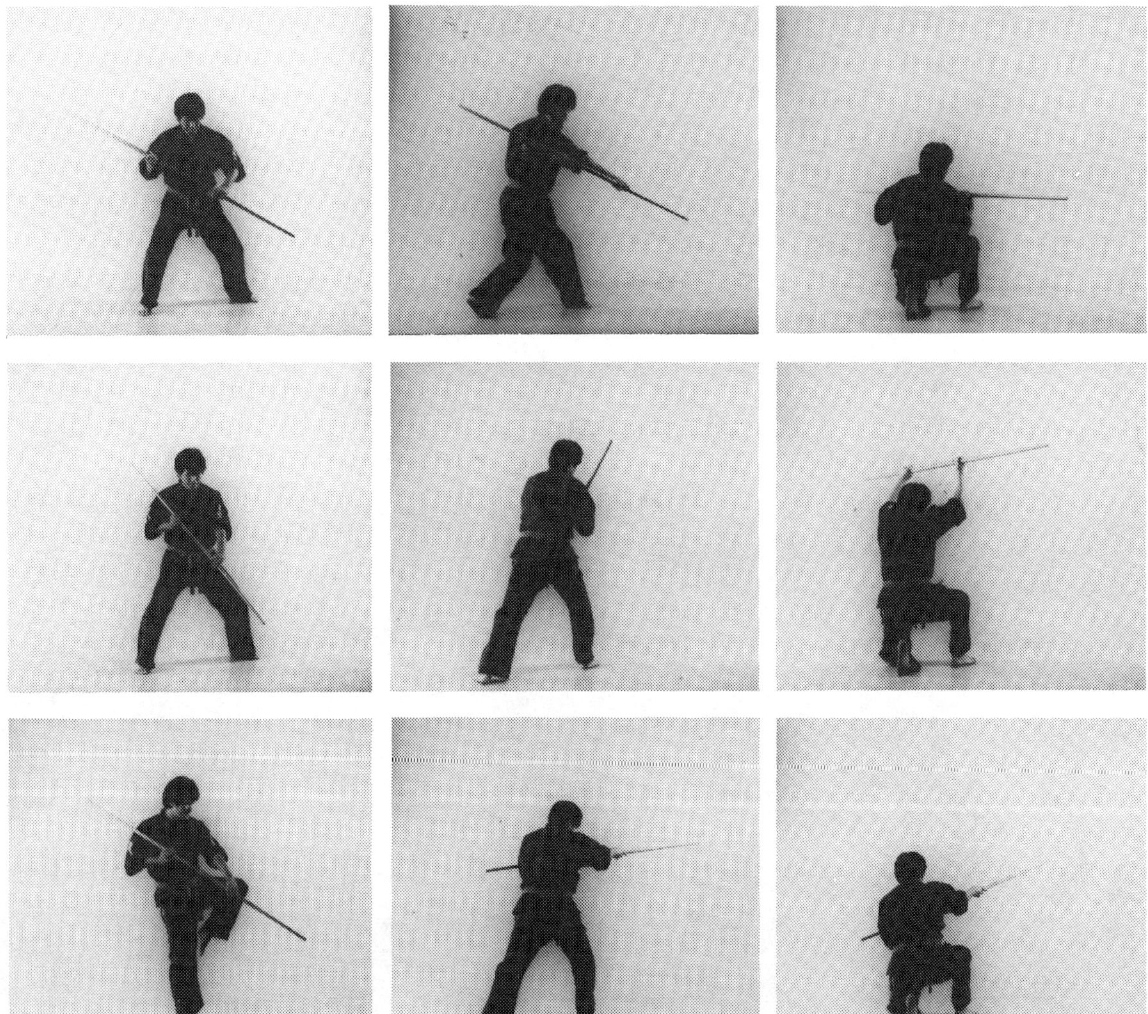

37. Pull back into a middle block.
38. Follow with a poke strike.
39. Stand and turn 180 degrees counterclockwise.
40. Prepare to strike.
41. Twist your body into a right-hand strike.
42. Recoil for a middle block.
43. Block your opponent's strike.
44. Drop bo into strike position.
45. Step forward and prepare to strike.

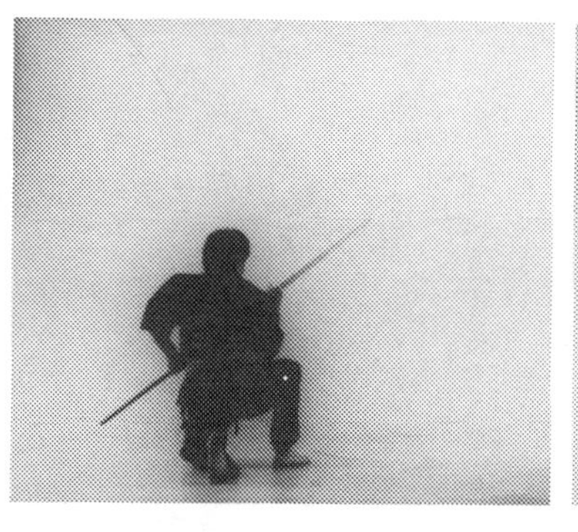

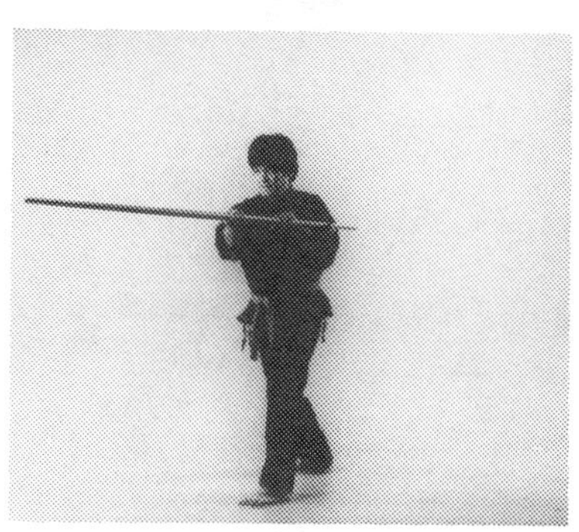

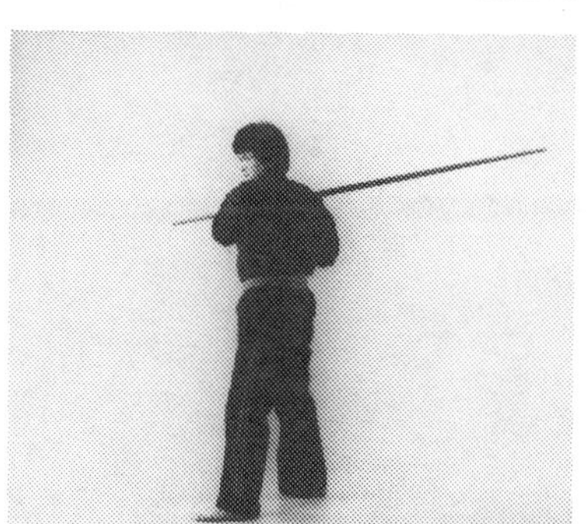

46. Follow with right-hand strike.
47. Pull back for middle block.
48. Move right foot back.

49. Jump back.
50. Prepare for middle block.
51. Prepare to strike.

52. Step forward and follow with right-hand strike.
53. Turn 180 degrees counterclockwise.
54. Follow with a low block.

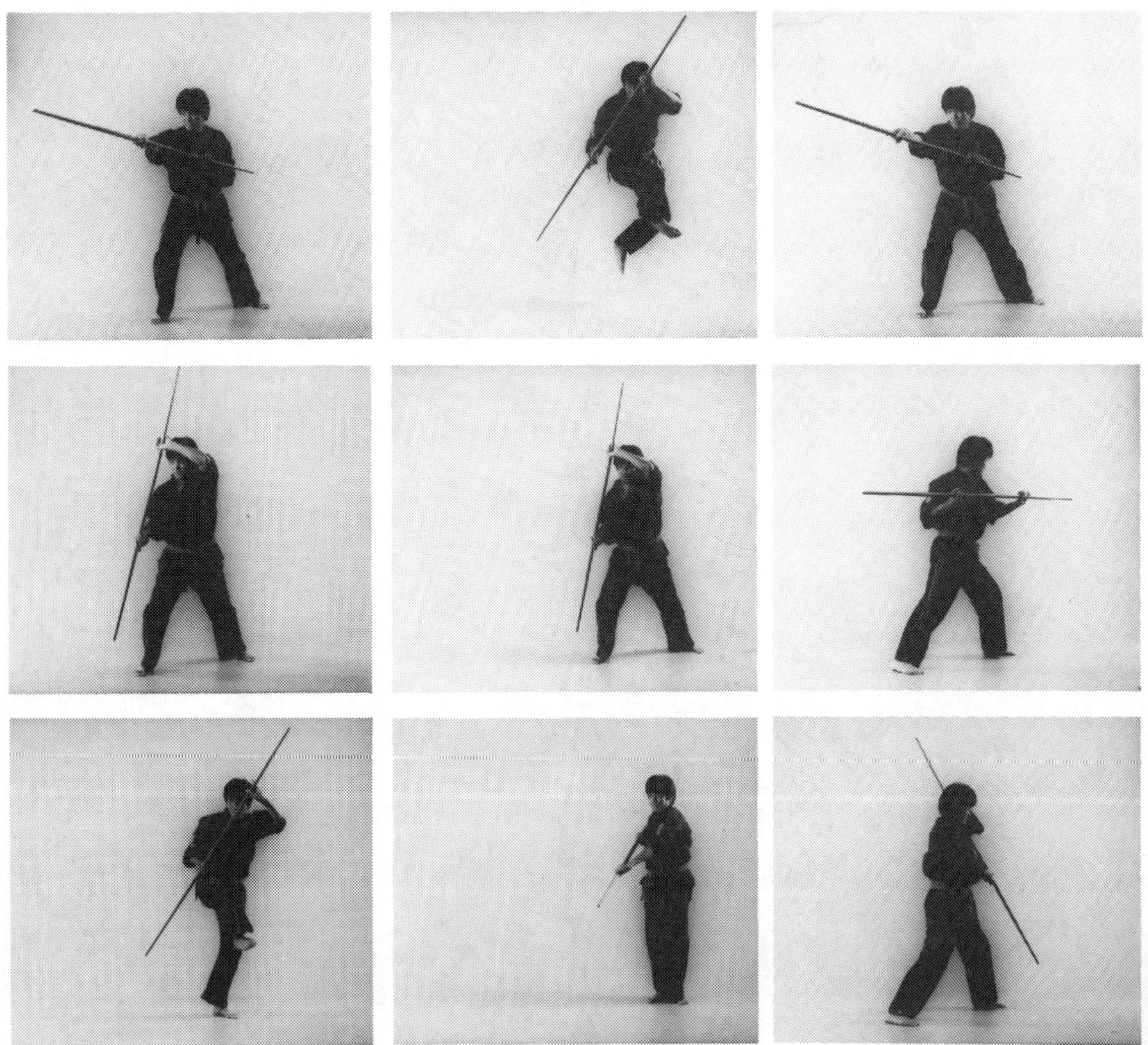

55. Bring feet together and apply a lower block.
56. Prepare for downward strike.
57. Strike down and turn 180 degrees counterclockwise.
58. Assume a cat stance, ready to flick sand.
59. Flick bo.
60. Recoil into middle block.
61. Thrust forward.
62. Bring right foot back, bo at right side.
63. Step to the side with your left foot.
64. End in upright position with bo at your side.

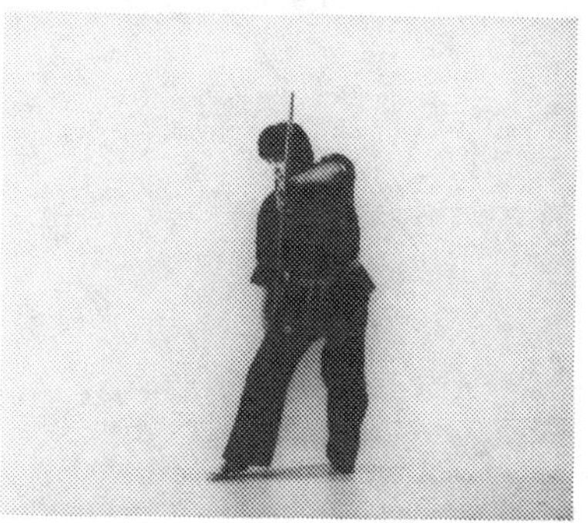

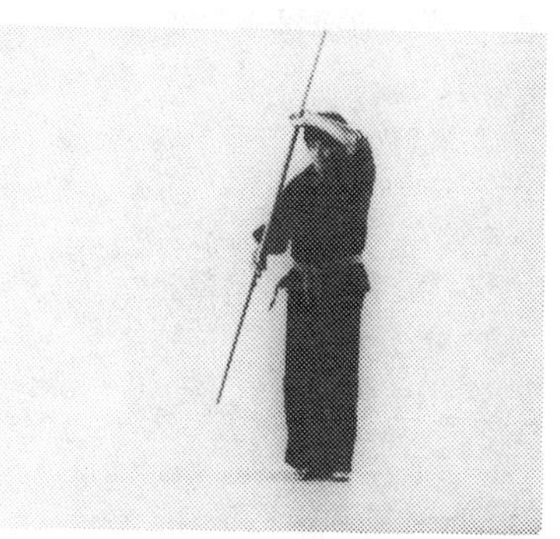

Tsuken No Kun

1. Begin from a natural stance.
2. Assume a ready position for the kata.
3. Step back with the left leg.
4. Strike while in right front stance.
5. Block to the side.
6. Cross-step forward.
7. Step forward.
8. Strike forward in right front stance.
9. Turn 180 degrees counterclockwise and block.

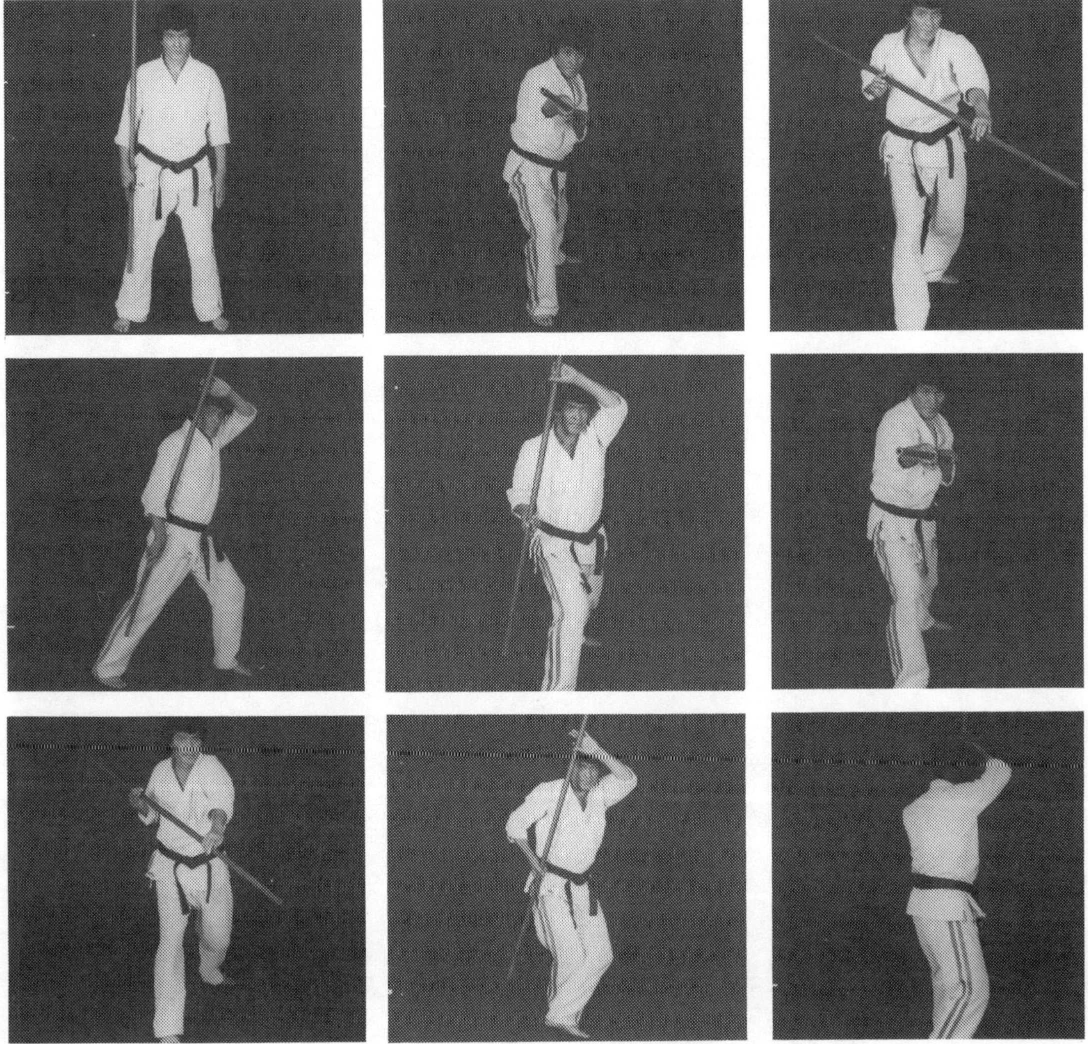

10. Cross-step forward.
11. Strike forward in left front stance.
12. Turn 180 degrees counterclockwise and block while in cat stance.
13. Move into front stance.
14. Strike forward.
15. Step forward into left front stance.
16. Swing rear end of bo and strike.
17. Step forward.
18. Strike while in right front stance.

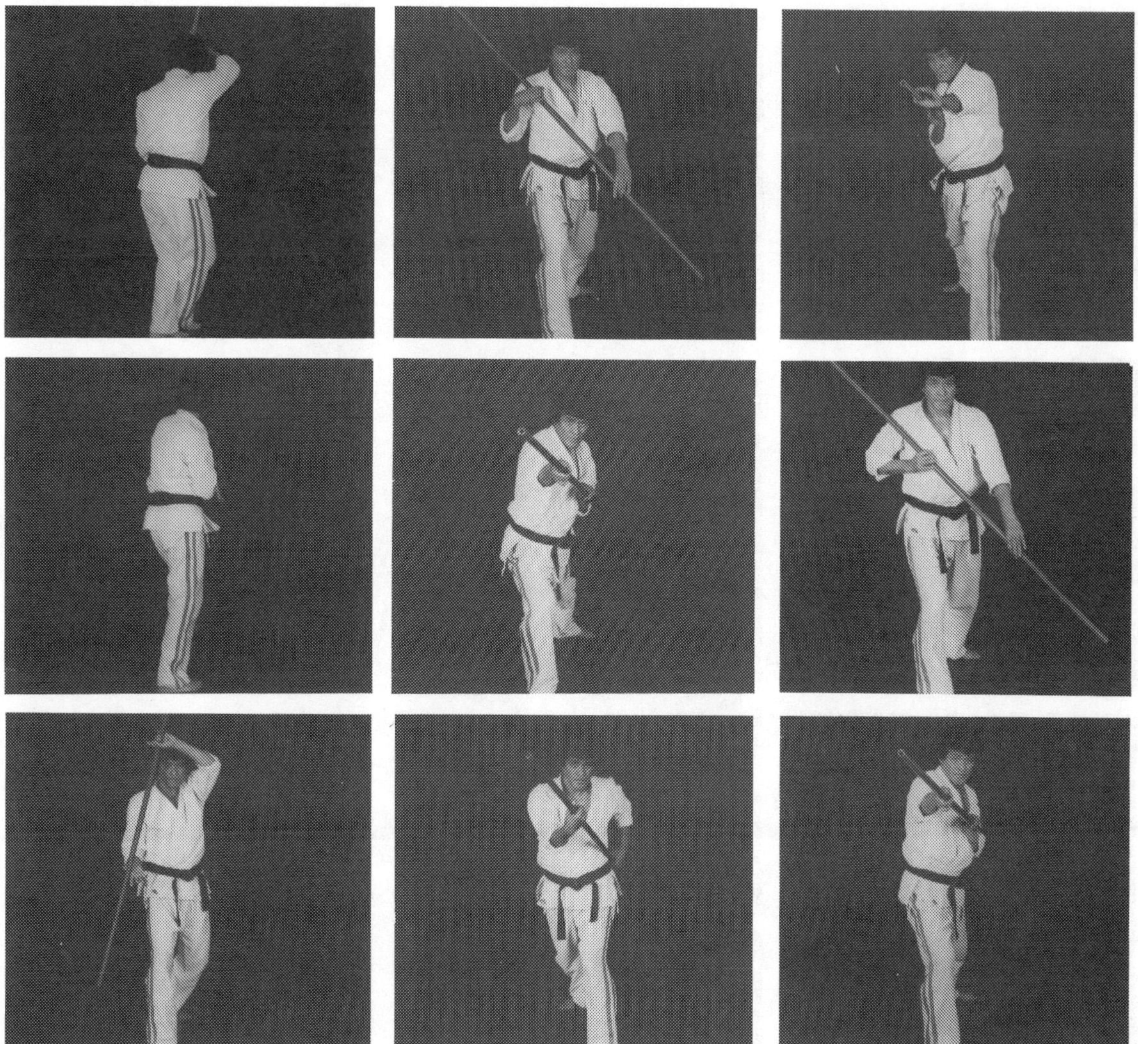

19. From a cat stance execute an outside block.
20. Poke the bo forward.
21. Pivot on your right foot.
22. And swing the bo counterclockwise.
23. Step forward.
24. Strike forward.
25. Pivot on your left foot.
26. Swing the bo counterclockwise.
27. Switch grips and raise the bo.

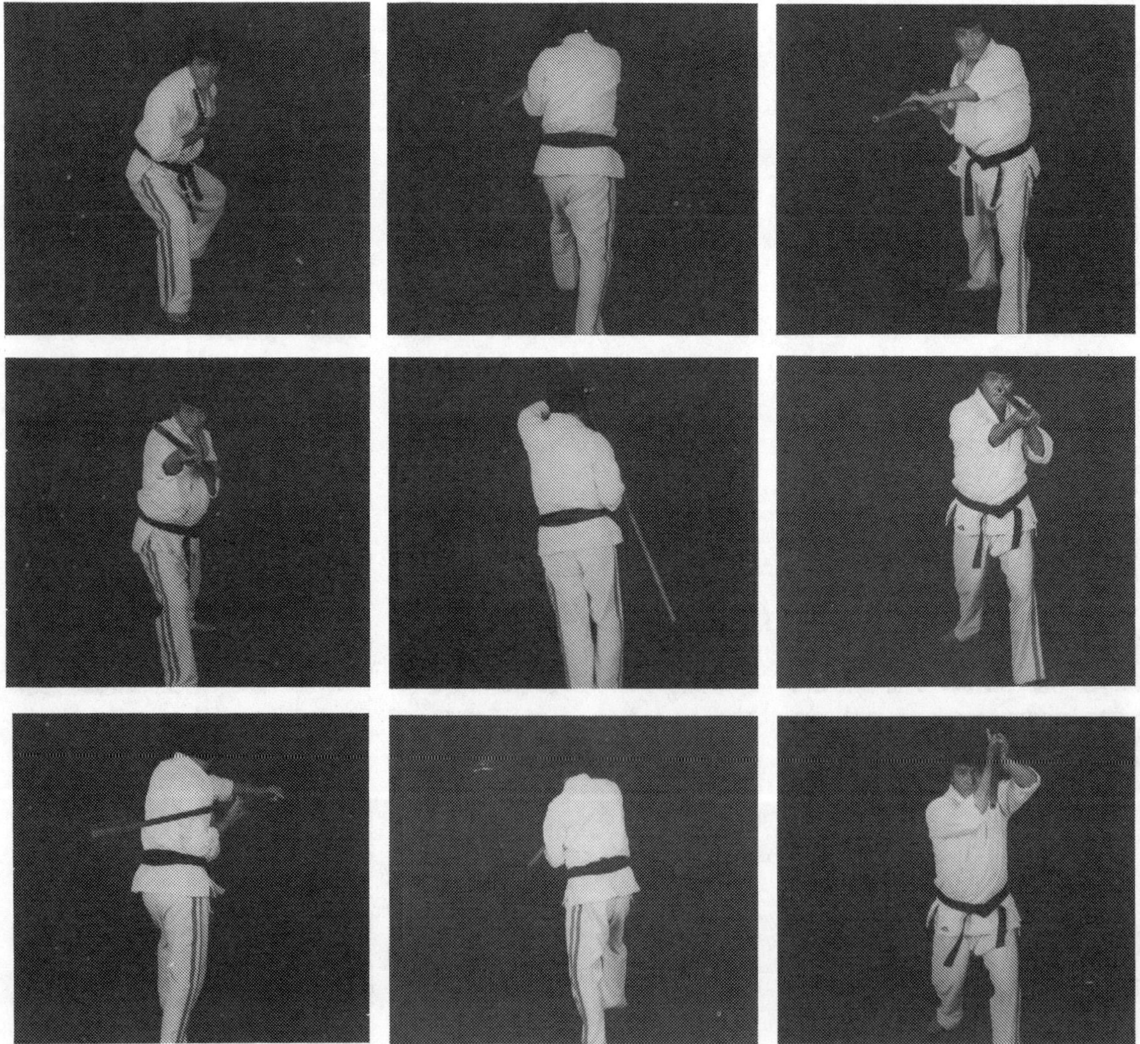

28. Bring up right foot.
29. Step forward and strike.
30. Assume horse stance and strike left.
31. Swing the bo clockwise to your side.
32. Unwind the swing.
33. Strike to the side.
34. Step 180 degrees to your left.
35. Step forward and strike.
36. Move into a cat stance and form an outside block.

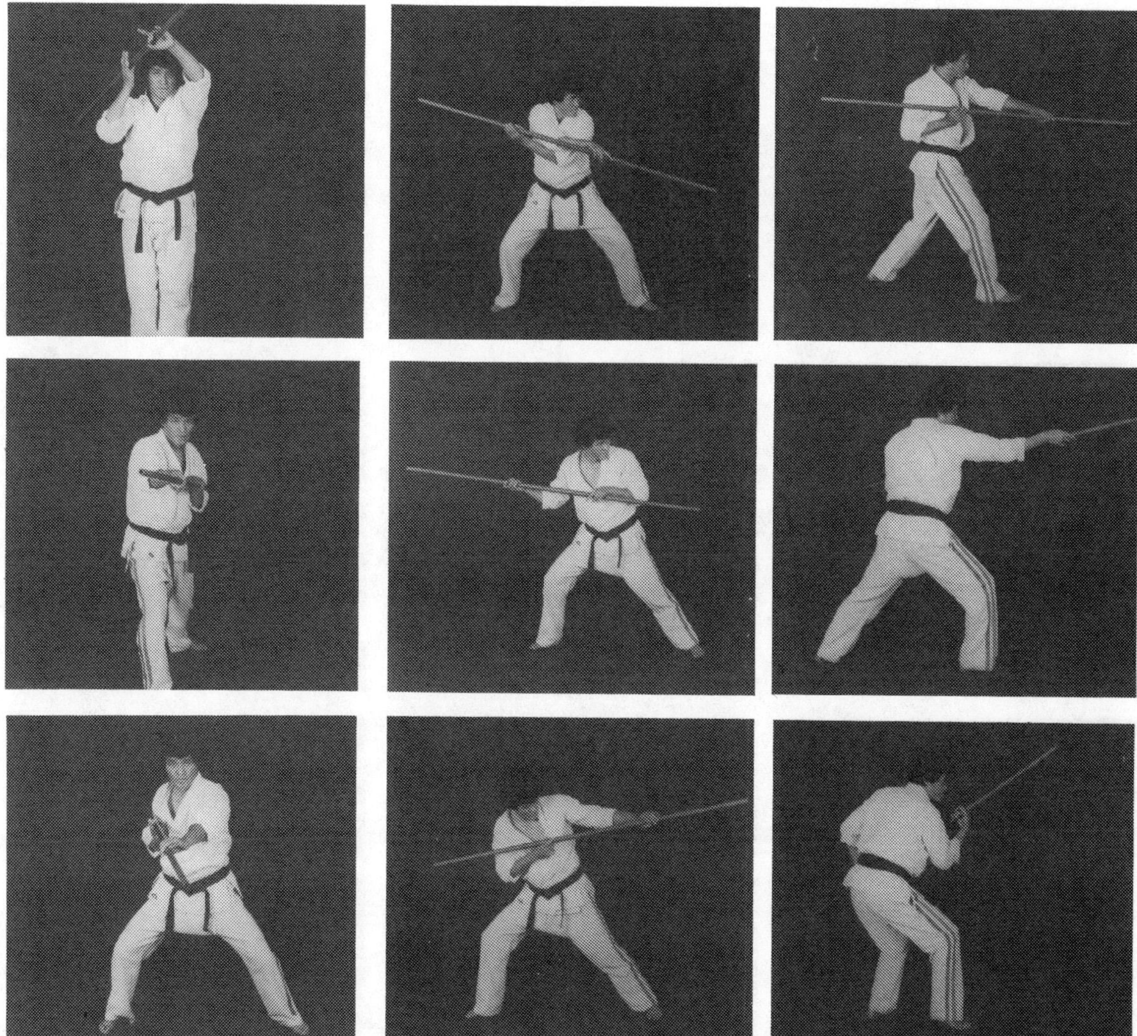

37. Step forward and strike.
38. Pull in the bo.
39. Spin clockwise 180 degrees.
40. Swing the bo clockwise to your side.
41. Unwind the swing.
42. Strike to the left side.
43. Step forward.
44. Strike forward.
45. Pull back into an outside block.

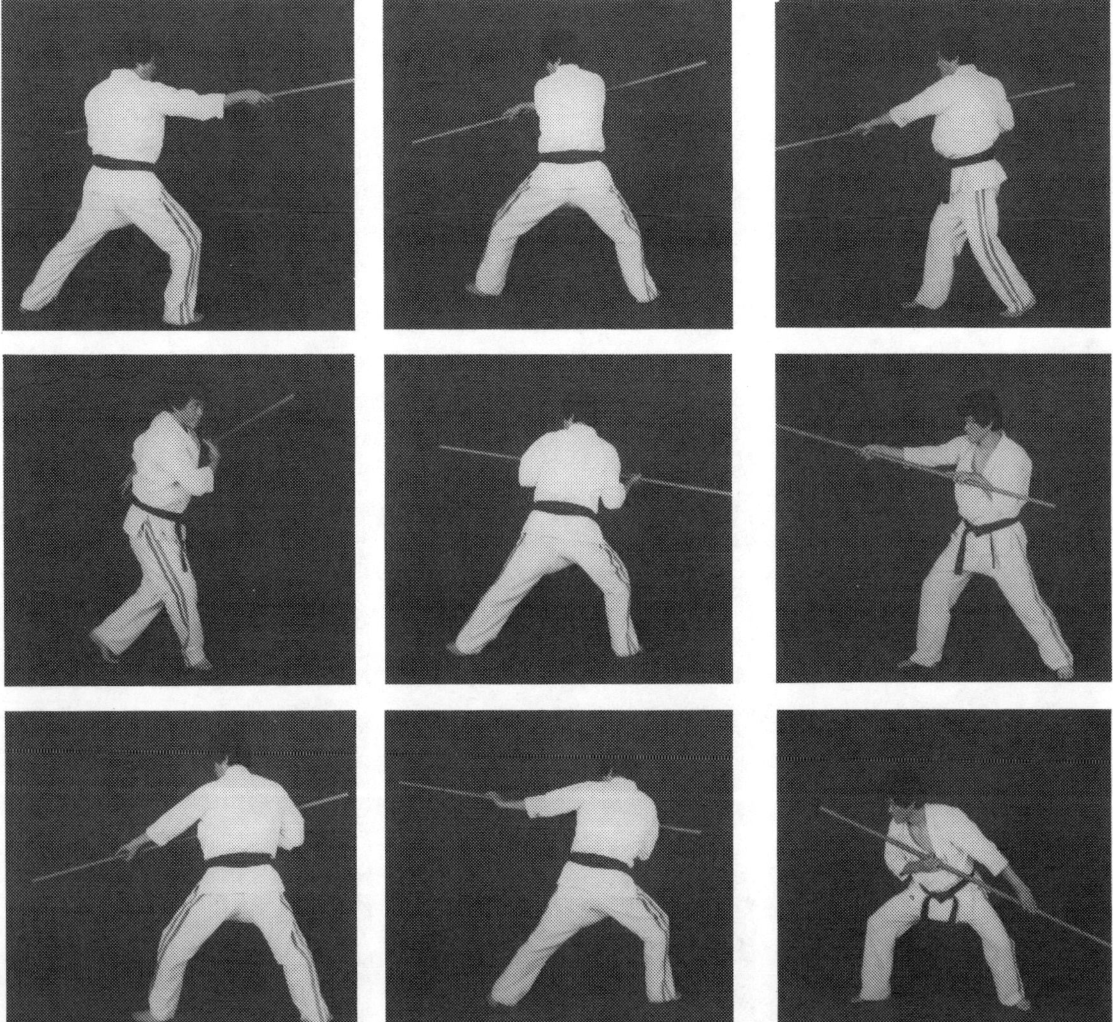

46. Strike again from a front stance.
47. Move into an outside block from a cat stance.
48. Return to original direction.
49. Step forward.
50. Strike forward.
51. Move into an outside block from a cat stance.
52. Strike forward again.
53. Spin counterclockwise.
54. Lift left leg.

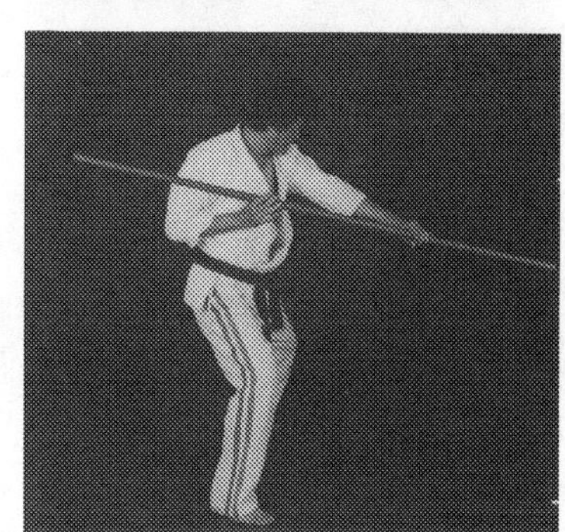

55. Lower left leg.
56. Strike forward right.
57. Get into a horse stance for an outside block.
58. Strike again.
59. In a cat stance, block to the left.
60. Lift the lower portion of the bo.
61. Block down.
62. Step forward and strike.
63. From a cat stance, move to an outside block.

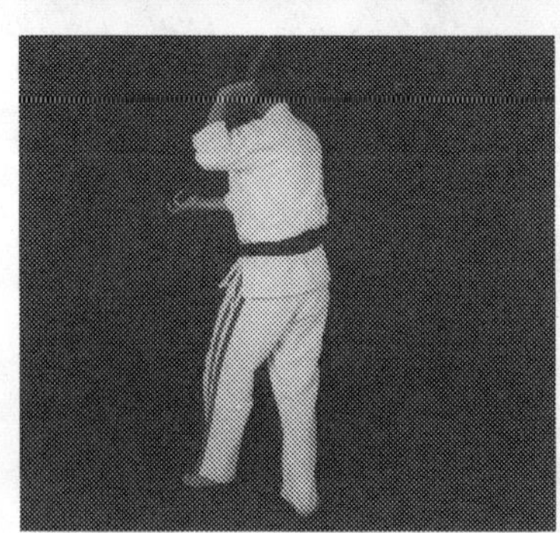

64. Strike forward.
65. Pivot 180 degrees counterclockwise.
66. Face forward and strike low.
67. Step back with left leg.
68. Strike while in right front stance.
69. Pull back to natural stance.

BOJUTSU POSITIONS

No study of the bo would be complete without a discussion of the *kamae* or traditional positions and postures through which all other movements are made. A perfect kamae combines mental, physical and emotional skills, all equally important in the overall success of the motion. To master just one element leaves the practitioner open in two other areas. A bojutsu artist may have the physical skills, but still lack essential tools in the mental and emotional areas. Thus, his readiness and energy levels fall short.

The five basic bo postures include: chudan-kamae; gedan-kamae; jodan-kamae; waki-kamae; and hasso-kamae.

Chudan-Kamae — In this posture, the right hand is extended and the left hand is positioned toward the back of the body. Both legs are bent, with the right foot out and the left back.

Gedan-Kamae — More commonly known as the "cat stance," the weight is on the heels of the practitioner. The right knee is out and the left hand is raised. The right hand is down, with both palms facing the floor. The fingers are tight, as though gripping the bo.

Jodan-Kamae — The practitioner has both hands up and his fingers tight and curled. His right hand is turned over and behind his head while his left hand is straight out from his chin. His elbow is bent at a 45-degree angle.

Waki-Kamae — The right arm is bent and crosses but does not touch the chest. The left hand is tight and placed behind the right hip.

Hasso-Kamae — The body is turned in a 45-degree angle. The left arm is back and extended, while the right arm is out to the side. The elbow is bent and the fists are turned toward the sky.

BO APPLICATIONS

The true worth of any kata is determined by how well it works in an actual fighting situation. In the following sequences, you will see how effective the bo and its sister weapons can be in combat applications.

The attacker attempts (1) to strike with an upper thrust, but the defender, in a cat stance, successfully blocks (2) the blow. The attacker makes (3) another attempt, but the defender uses the maneuverability (4) of his cat stance to defend himself.

As the attacker swings (1) his bo around his head, the defender steps into a front stance. The attacker attempts (2) a right-hand strike, but the defender steps (3) back 45 degrees into a cat stance to block the blow.

The attacker raises (1) his bo before moving into a right-hand strike. The defender, however, is ready with a side block (2).

The attacker swings (1) his bo counterclockwise and attempts a downward strike (2). The defender blocks (3) the blow with a downward block.

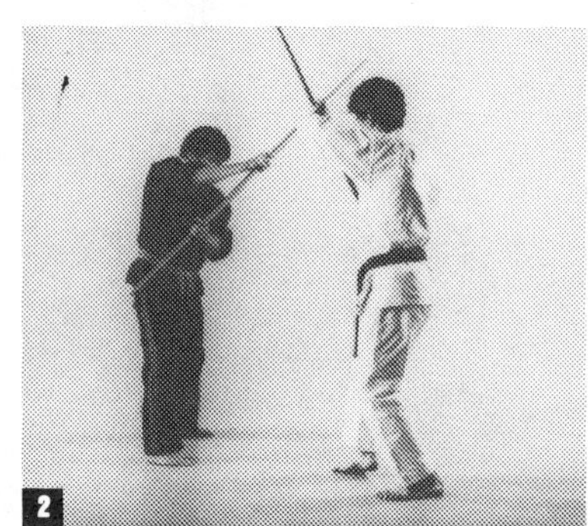

The attacker raises (1) his bo, but the defender sets himself by stepping (2) forward and raising his bo over his head. His high block (3) thwarts the downward strike.

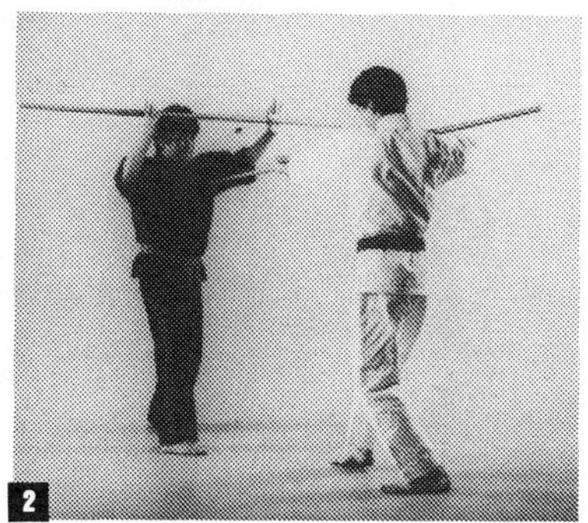

The attacker is stopped by a middle block, as the defender steps forward and lowers his bo.

The attacker attempts to strike (1) at the knee, but the defender uses (2) a low block to stop the intended blow.

The defender stops (1) the thrust with a side block.

1

The attacker swings (1) his bo for a blow to the head, but the defender steps into a cat stance and executes (2) an outside block.

1

2

The attacker steps (1) forward and attempts a downward strike (2). The defender blocks the blow and swings (3) the top end of the bo up.

1

2

3

The attacker attempts a shoulder strike (1), but the defender thwarts the blow by having his bo against (2) the left side of the body.

The defender steps sideways and hooks the attacker's bo.

The attacker moves (1) in for a low strike, but the defender steps into a cat stance and uses a side block to push away the blow (2).

As the attacker approaches (1), the defender steps back (2) and sets his bo for the block. A right-side block (3) eliminates the danger.

As the attacker steps (1) forward the defender steps back. The defender counters with a strike (2) to the knee, but the blow is stopped with a low block (3).

The attacker attempts (1) to strike with the lower end of his bo. The defender stops one blow (2) with a middle block and then thwarts a right-hand strike (3) with a high block.

The attacker (1) sets for a strike to the head, but the defender is ready (2) with a high block.

The attacker attempts (1) a left-hand strike, but the defender pushes the bo clockwise. The attacker recoils (2) for a downward strike, but the defender is ready (3) with a low block.

Continuing the blocking motion, the man on the left pushes (1) down his opponent's bo. He then tries to sweep (2) his enemy's legs. The defender avoids (3) the sweep by jumping, lands and attempts (4) a forward thrust. The thrust is blocked as the defender steps into a cat stance and blocks with the side of the bo (5).

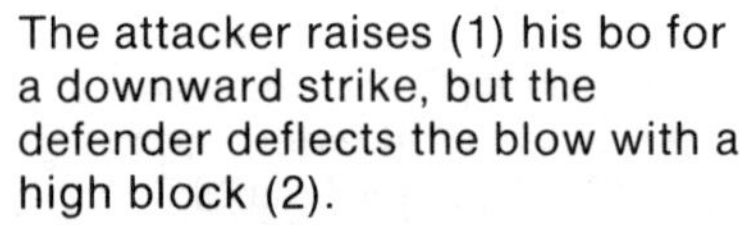
The attacker raises (1) his bo for a downward strike, but the defender deflects the blow with a high block (2).

The attacker strikes to the side (1), but the defender blocks the blow by holding the bo against the side of his arm (2).

The attacker pulls (1) back and tries to strike the defender's midsection. The defender steps (2) away into a cat stance and makes the blow (3) miss him.

The attacker throws (1) his bo at the defender to confuse him. While the defender is ducking (2), the attacker grabs (3) his enemy's bo.

The attacker immobilizes the defender by grabbing his bo (1), and then strikes (2) him in the head with a right-hand blow. The enemy falls (3) to the ground.

From the ready position (1), the attacker strikes at the knee. The defender blocks with a low block (2), but the attacker recoils (3) and attempts another low strike (4). The defender stops the blow with the lower portion of his bo (5).

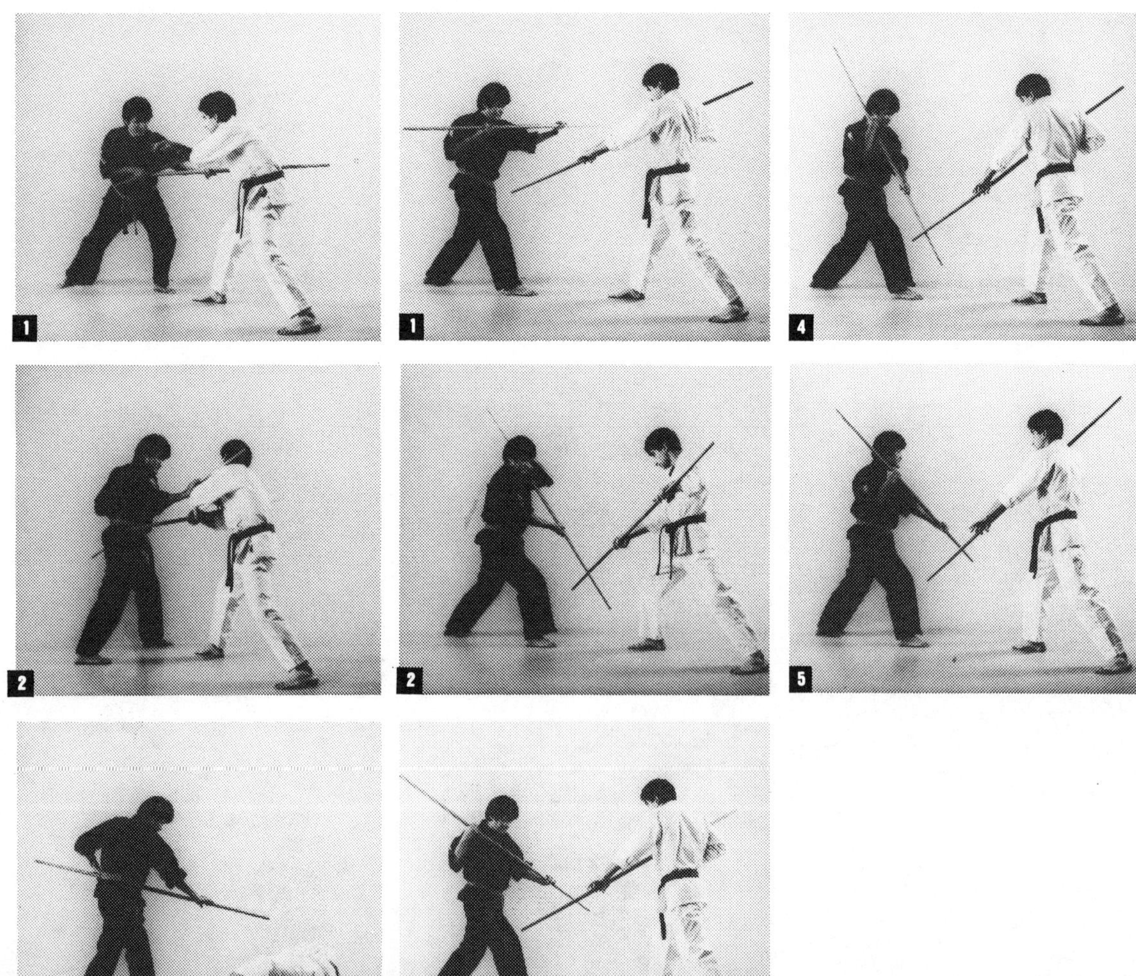

The attacker strikes to the head (1), but the defender deflects the blow with a side block.

1

The attacker attempts a forward thrust (1), but the defender successfully thwarts the blow with a block to the side (2).

1

2

The attacker strikes (1-3) at his enemy's knee by stepping forward and hitting with the lower end of the bo. The defender deflects the blow by stepping back and blocking with the lower end of his bo.

1

2

3

The attacker (1) pokes at his foe's foot, but the defender pushes away the blow with a low block (2).

The attacker attempts a strike (1) to the head. The defender, however, uses an inside block with the upper end of the bo to thwart the move (2).

The attacker moves in for a strike by stepping forward (1), but the defender (2) steps back and blocks the blow with the lower end of the bo.

The attacker tries to strike his enemy again (1) by stepping forward, but the defender avoids the blow by stepping back and thrusting with the upper end of his bo (2).

The attacker steps up (1) and tries to strike the defender with the lower end of his bo (2). But the defender steps back (3) and lifts his leg, making the blow miss (4). He then drops his leg and blocks (5) the blow with the lower portion of his bo.

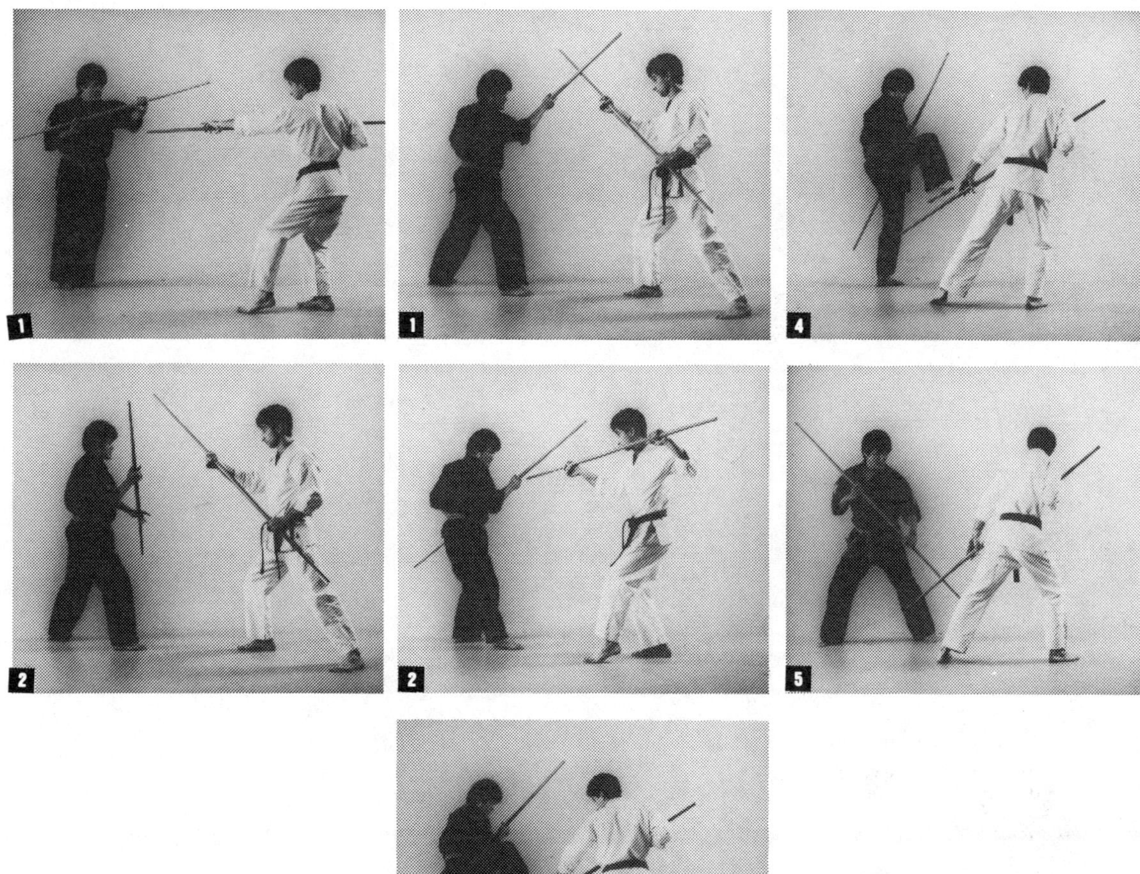

The attacker steps forward (1) and attempts to strike. The defender steps back to block the attempt (2), and is in position (3) to block a right-hand strike.

The attacker shows he is about to attempt a downward strike (1). The defender goes down on one knee (2). As the attacker strikes down (3), the defender raises (4) his bo over his head for an upper block.

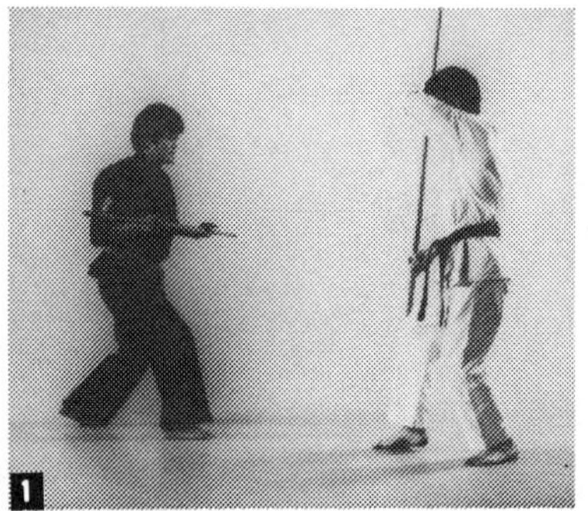

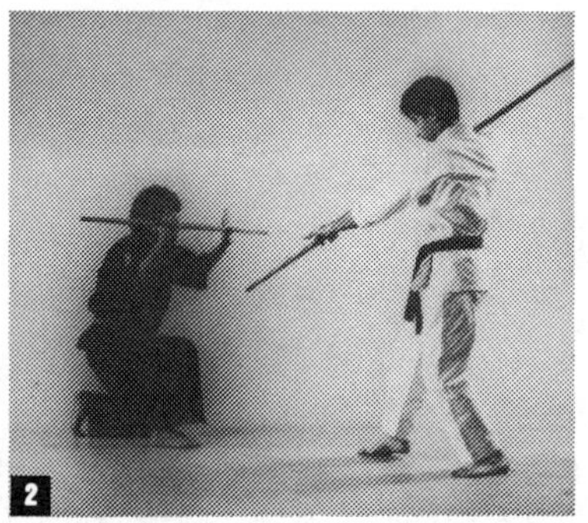

While on one knee, the defender turns (1) to the offensive strike, but the blow is thwarted by an outside block (2).

The attacker attempts a forward thrust (1), but the defender deflects the blow with an outside block (2).

As the attacker strikes again (1), the defender is equal to the task by executing an outside block (2).

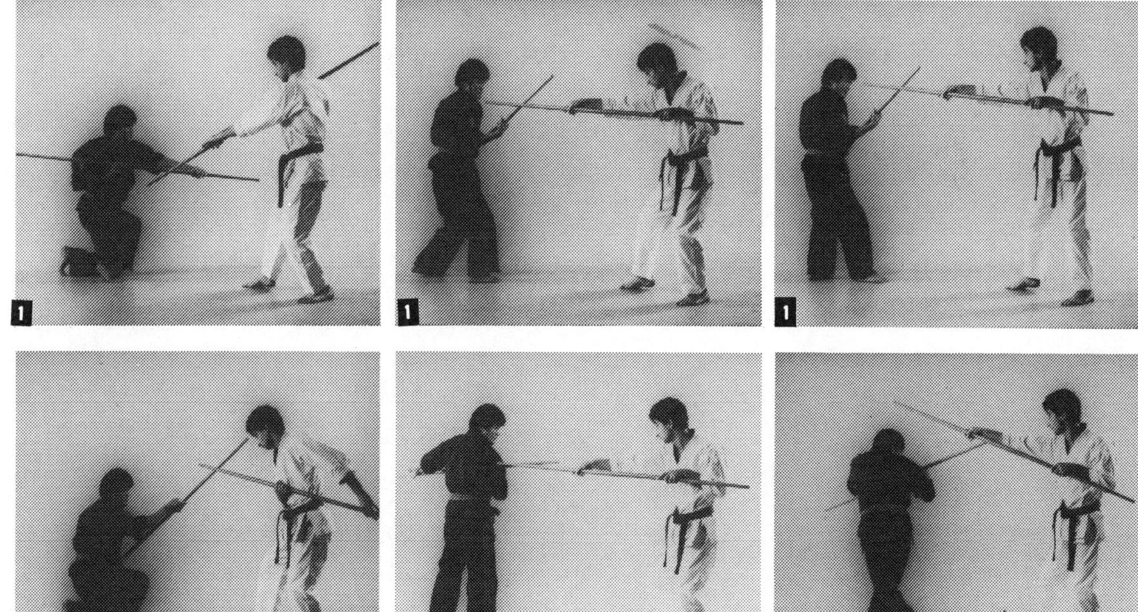

The attacker spins (1) counterclockwise and strikes at the knee area. The defender blocks the blow (2) with the lower end of his bo.

The defender (right) blocks the blow by swinging (1-3) his opponent's bo in a clockwise direction.

The attacker strikes (1) by thrusting at his opponent's knee. While in a cat stance (2), the defender blocks the thrust with a side move.

As the attacker attempts a strike to the head (1), the defender blocks the blow with the upper end of his bo.

While swinging the bo counterclockwise over his head (1), the attacker moves into a position for a strike at the knee (2). The defender uses a side block (3) to stop the blow.

As the attacker strikes to the head (1), the defender stops the blow with the upper end of his bo (2).

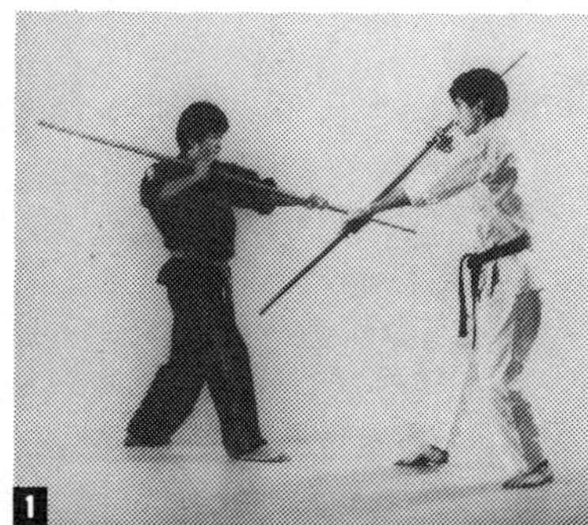

As the attacker strikes toward the knee with the upper end of his bo (1), the defender gets into a cat stance and blocks (2) the blow with the upper end of his weapon.

The attacker pushes his enemy's bo to the side (1) and tries to strike him at the knees. The defender, however, blocks the attempt with the lower end of his bo (2).

1

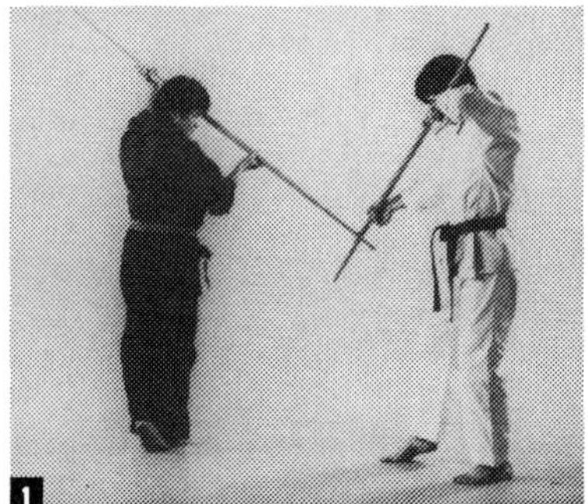

1

2

2

Finishing off the application sets (1-4), both practitioners simultaneously do outside blocks. They end by touching weapons in the middle.

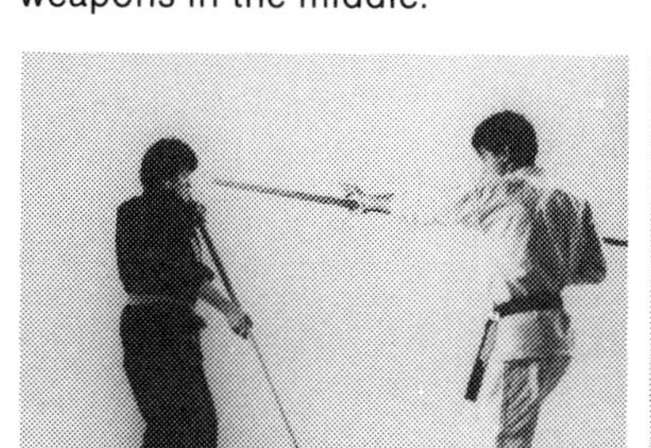

1

2

3

4

When you are done (1), pull away and bow to show respect (2).

1

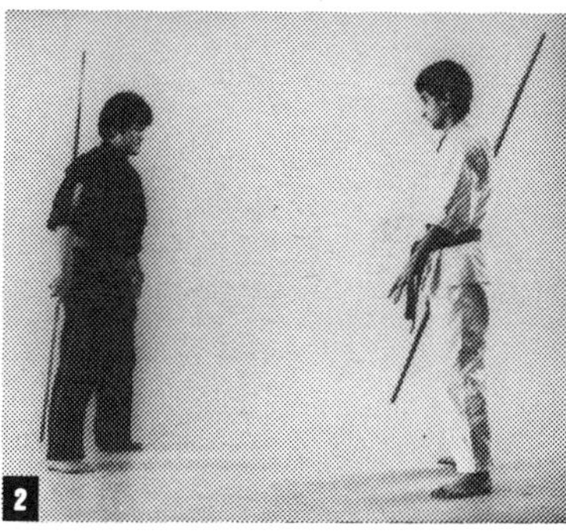

2

Defenses against the bo

The attacker grabs (1) the bo, but the defender swings the bo clockwise (2). The defender pushes the bo down (3) over the attacker's head and he falls (4) to the ground.

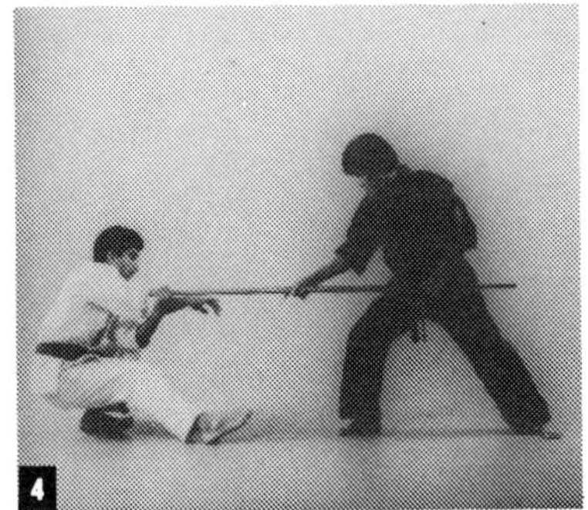

The attacker grabs the bo (1), but the defender swings the bo counterclockwise (2). The defender then pushes the bo (3) over the attacker's body and he falls to the ground (4).

The attacker grabs the bo (1), but the defender swings the bo counterclockwise (2). The defender then steps (3) through under the bo, which throws the attacker off balance (4). The defender pushes his enemy (5) off balance and he falls (6) to the ground.

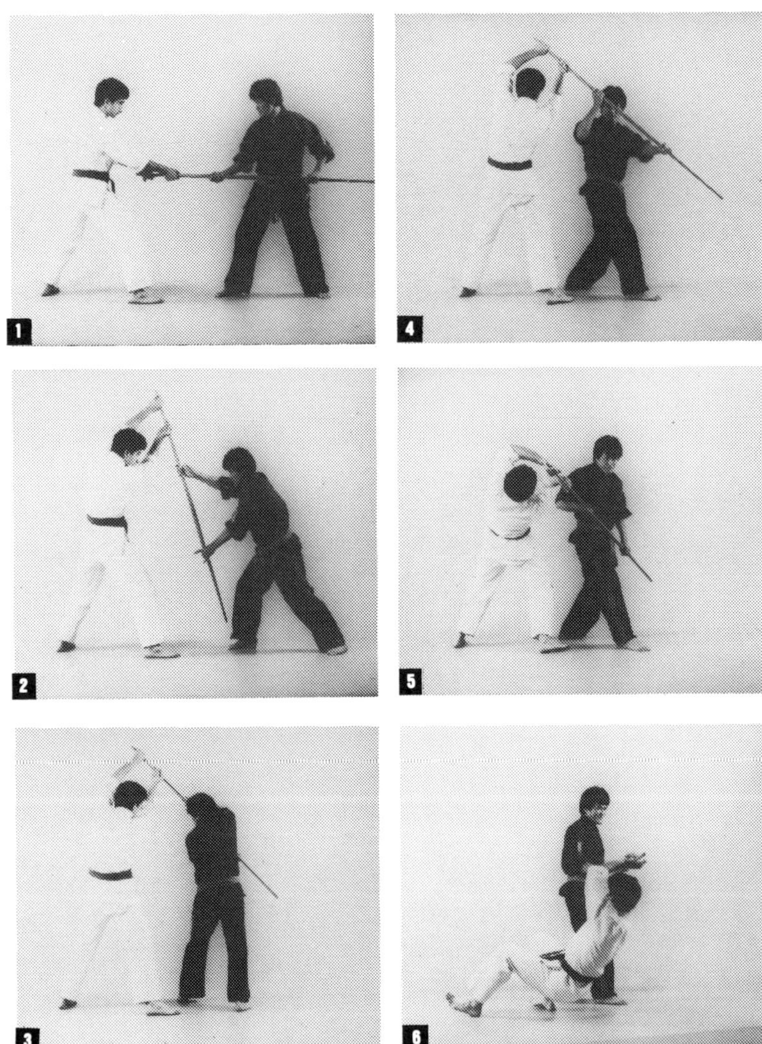

The attacker grabs his foe's wrist (1). The defender swings the bo counterclockwise (2), which locks up his attacker's wrist (3). The defender then pushes down on the arm (4) while holding the lock. He then strikes his attacker in the face (5) with the bo.

The attacker grabs his enemy's wrist (1), but the defender swings the bo around his attacker's wrist (2). The defender pushes down the attacker by tugging on the bo (3).

The attacker grabs the defender's wrist (1), but the defender swings the bo around his enemy's wrist (2). The defender then pushes down the attacker by bringing down the bo (3). The defender pushes his attacker back (4-6) by shoving the bo against his body.

The attacker grabs the bo with both hands (1). The defender swings the bo counterclockwise (2). He then brings the bo down so the attacker is off balance (3). He finishes him off by pushing him to the ground (4).

The attacker grabs the bo with both hands (1). The defender swings the bo counterclockwise (2). He keeps swinging until the attacker is off balance (3-4). Finally, he pushes the attacker to the ground (5).

The attacker grabs the bo (1). The defender steps forward with the bo (2), and hooks the bo around the attacker's neck (3). He then slides the bo between the attacker's legs (4), and pulls toward his body (5). This sends the attacker to the ground.

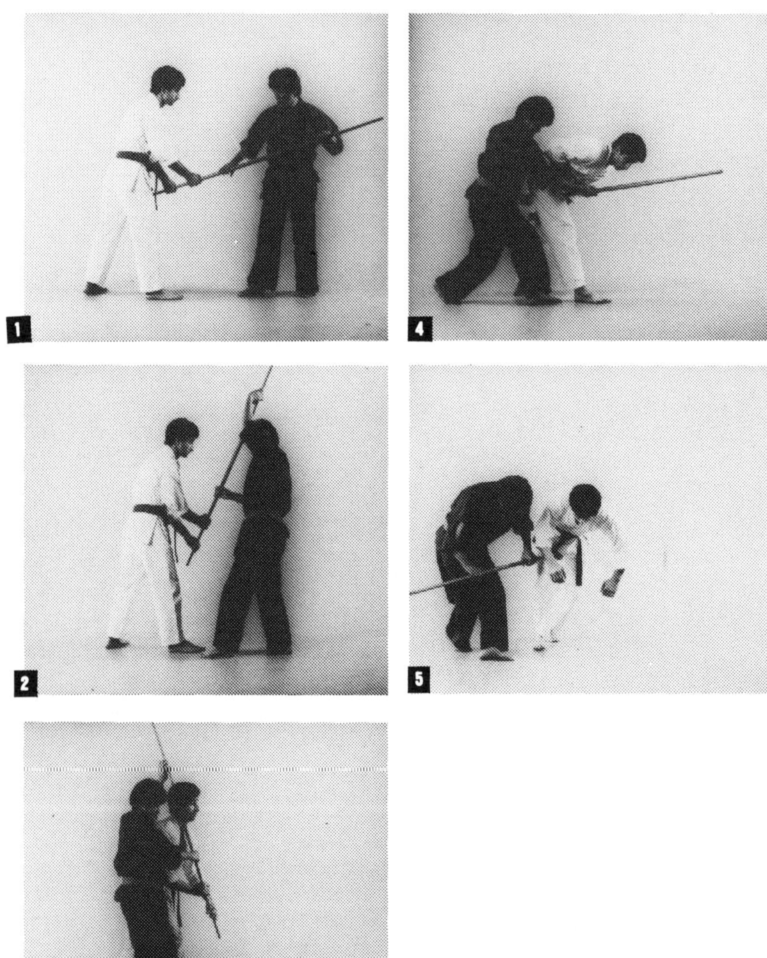

BASIC PREARRANGED BOJUTSU SPARRING TECHNIQUES

There are ten basic *kumite* prearranged sparring techniques associated with the art of bojutsu. They include: soto-uke; uchi-uke; sukai-uke; gedan-uke; harai-uke; jodan-uchi; hikkake A; gyaku hikkake B; gyaku hikkake C; and tai sabaki.

In all cases, the fighting techniques begin with the opponent's move. Once the attacker has shown his hand, the defender can use his bo to first fend off the attack and then move into an offensive mode.

In the soto-uke technique, the practitioner waits for an attack and then uses his bo to make an outer block. Once the block has been made, he follows with a well-placed thrust.

The uchi-uke is performed by taking the attacker inward before making the killing thrust. The sukai-uke features a sliding block followed by a back strike, while the gedan-uke blocks the opponent's blow toward the ground and makes an easy strike to the foot. In all instances, the defender's offensive move consumes little energy. Once his block has been made, he strikes a sensitive target area closest to his bo.

The harai-uke block takes the attacker's weapon away from his body in a round, scooping motion. The defender quickly adjusts and follows with a thrust. The jodan-uchi blocks an upward strike attempt and comes down with an overhead strike. The hikkake series (a-c) features round blocks followed by separate holds or strikes. In version A, the round block is followed by a turnaway move and a strike to any of several parts of the body. Once the round block is made in the gyaku hikkake, it is followed by an overhead push and a hold. The move in the gyaku hikkake is an overhead push followed by a strike. The tai sabaki technique includes a step to the side, a turning away of the weapon and finally a strike.

If an attack mode is better suited to victory, then the bojutsu practitioner has six options: nuki tsuki, which is a sliding thrust; maede tsuki, which is a front-hand thrust; gedan tsuki or low thrust; an overhead strike called jodan uchi; furiage uchi or upward strike; and ura uchi, which is a back strike.

BO COMBINATIONS

From the ready position (1), the attacker steps forward with his right foot and thrusts (2) the bo toward the defender's head. The defender, however, blocks (3) the intended blow with an upper block, recoils (4), and applies a punishing smash (5) to the side of the head.

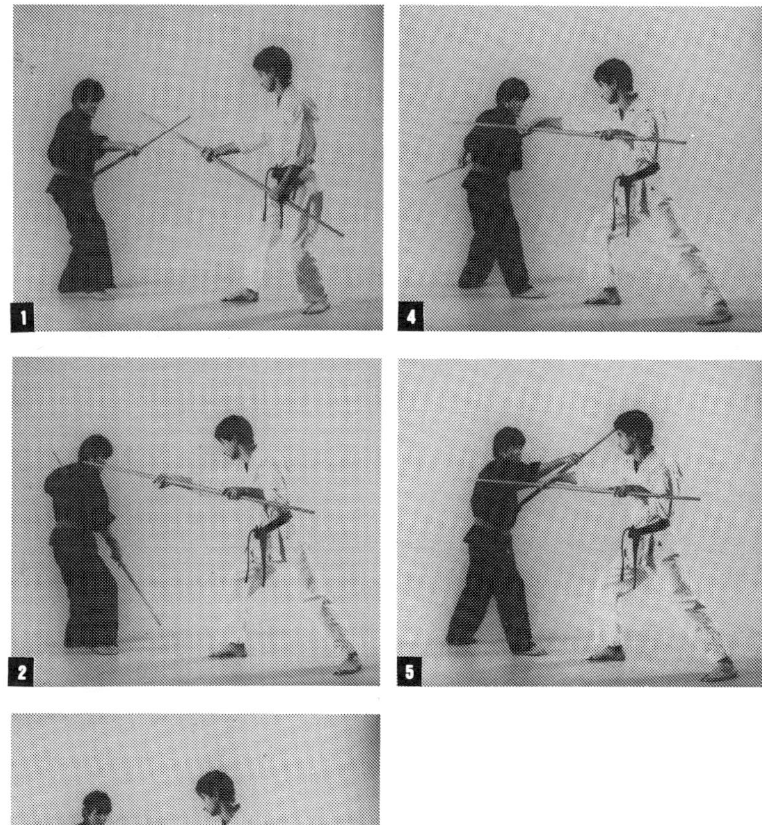

The attacker begins (1) with the bo over his head. He brings (2) it across his body and follows (3) with a right overhead smash.Thedefender uses an overhead block to stop the bo, shifts (4) his weight to his left side and slams the weapon into his opponent's ribs(5).

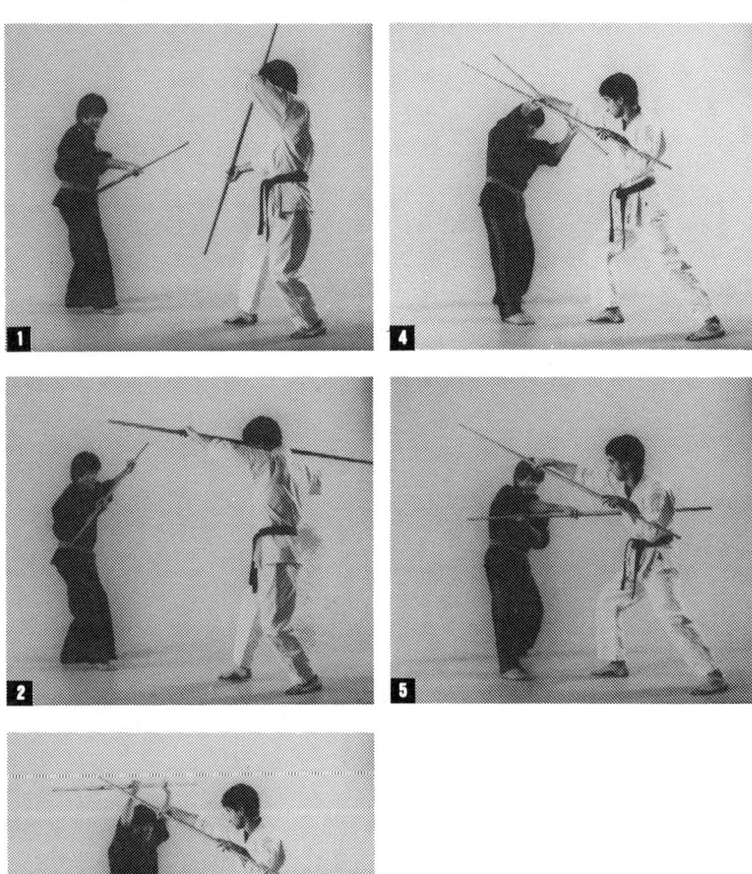

With the bo pointed (1) downward, the attacker lifts (2) the bo over his head and attempts a right downward strike. The defender (3) stops the blow with a simple overhead block, shifts the weight (4) to his left side and finishes (5) him off with a shot to the back and ribs.

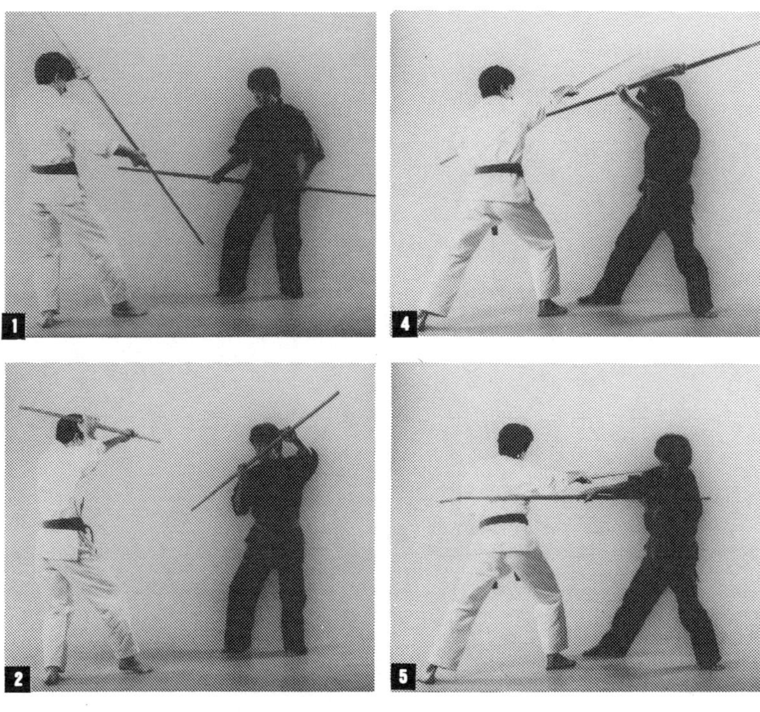

The attacker has his bo pointed (1) downward and follows with a low thrust (2) that is blocked at the ankles (3) by the defender. With his enemy out of the way, the defender pulls (4) up his bo and thrusts down (5) to smash the attacker's right foot.

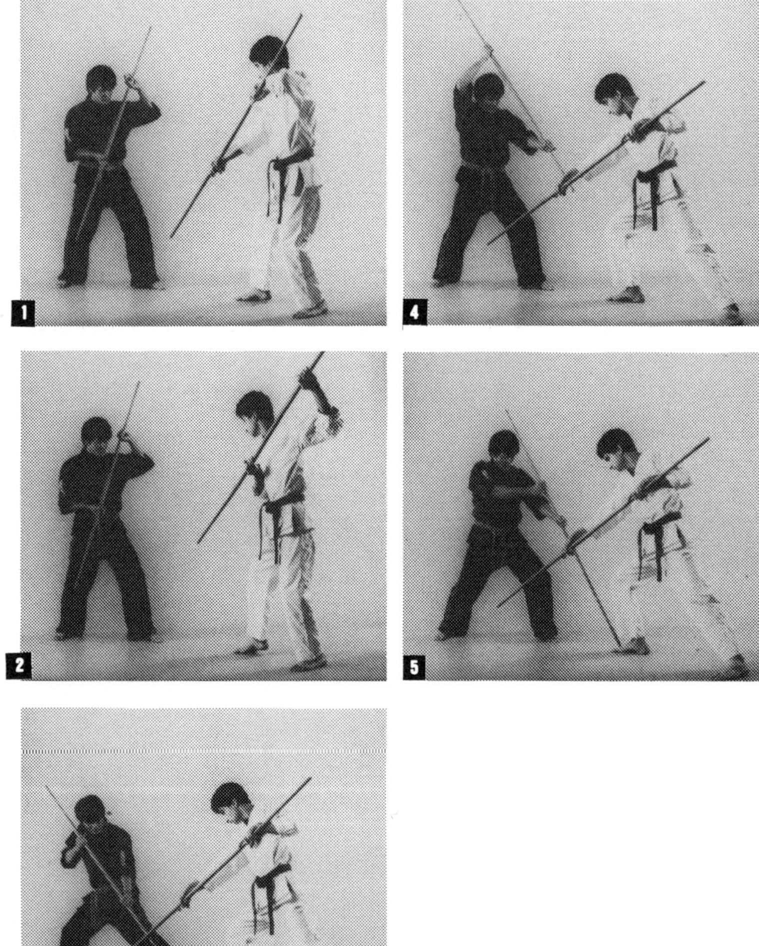

The defender's skill is put to the limit in this exchange (1). The attacker steps (2) back and thrusts (3) his bo toward the defender. Stepping (4) to his right, the defender blocks the surge and returns to his original position. The attacker repeats (5) the move and once again is rebuffed. This time, however, the defender recoils (6) and steps forward with his left foot for a left-hand smash (7) to the side of the head.

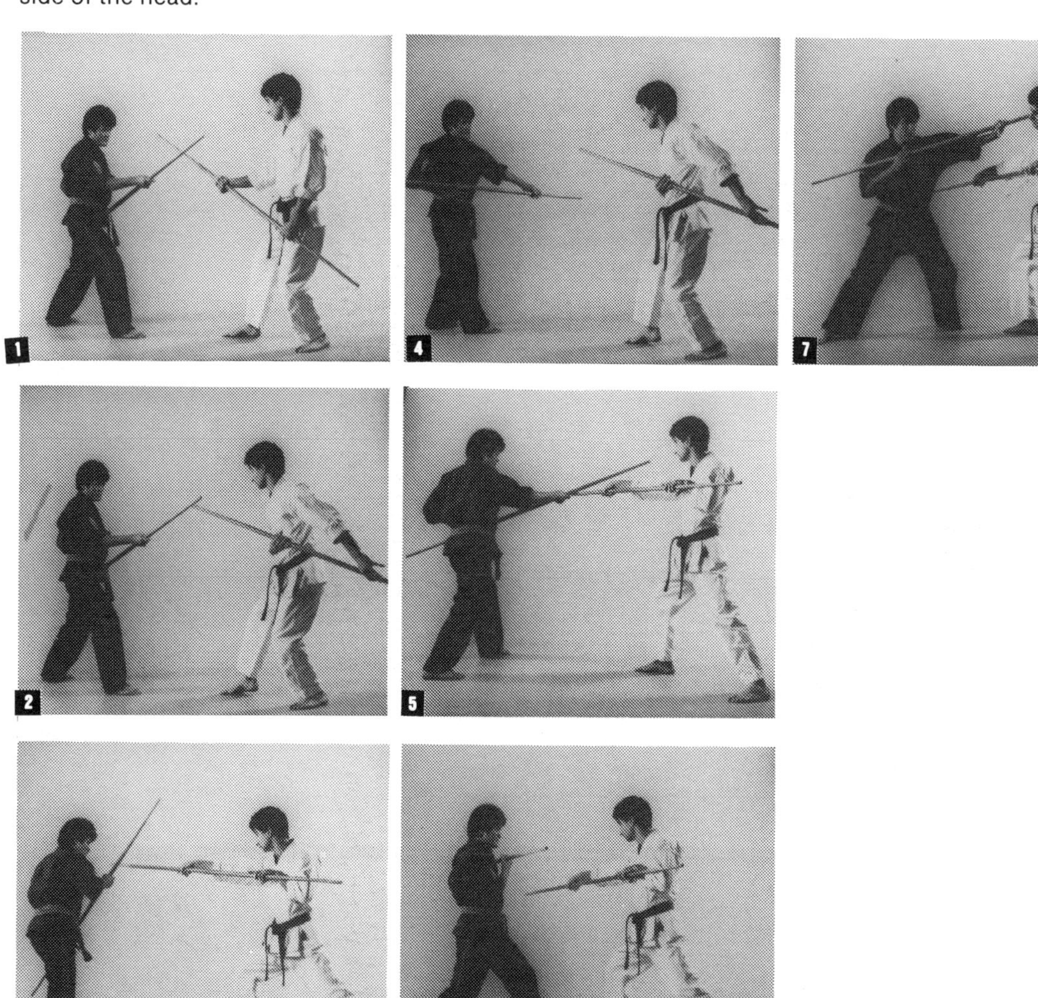

From a ready stance (1), the attacker steps forward (2) and thrusts his bo (3). The defender blocks the thrust to the side (4) and prepares to take the offensive (5). He grabs the bo (6) and pushes it off to the side (7) while ducking an upper thrust. He brings his bo down (8) for a strike to the head, and follows (9) by hooking his bo under the right arm of the attacker. He turns his wrist (10) and flips over the enemy (11).

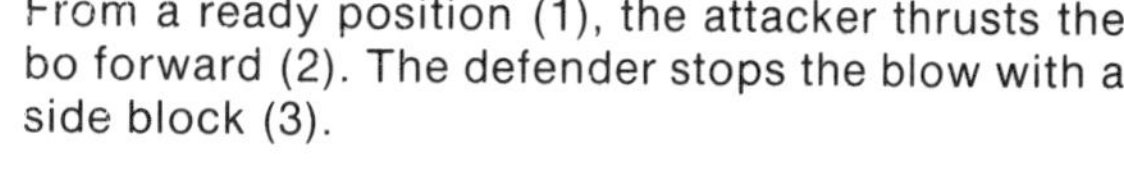
From a ready position (1), the attacker thrusts the bo forward (2). The defender stops the blow with a side block (3).

From a ready position (1), the attacker attempts a side thrust (2). The blow, however, is blocked to the side (3). Sensing an opening (4), the defender executes a right-hand strike (5) to the attacker's midsection. Powerless, the attacker doubles over (6) and is hit with a left-hand strike to the head (7). The defender recoils (8), and jabs the attacker in the ribs (9). He then lifts his bo (10) and comes over with a downward strike (11) to the head. He adds another jab in the ribs (12), recoils (13), strikes to the side of the head (14), pulls his bo back (15) and finishes off the attacker with a forward thrust to the stomach (16).

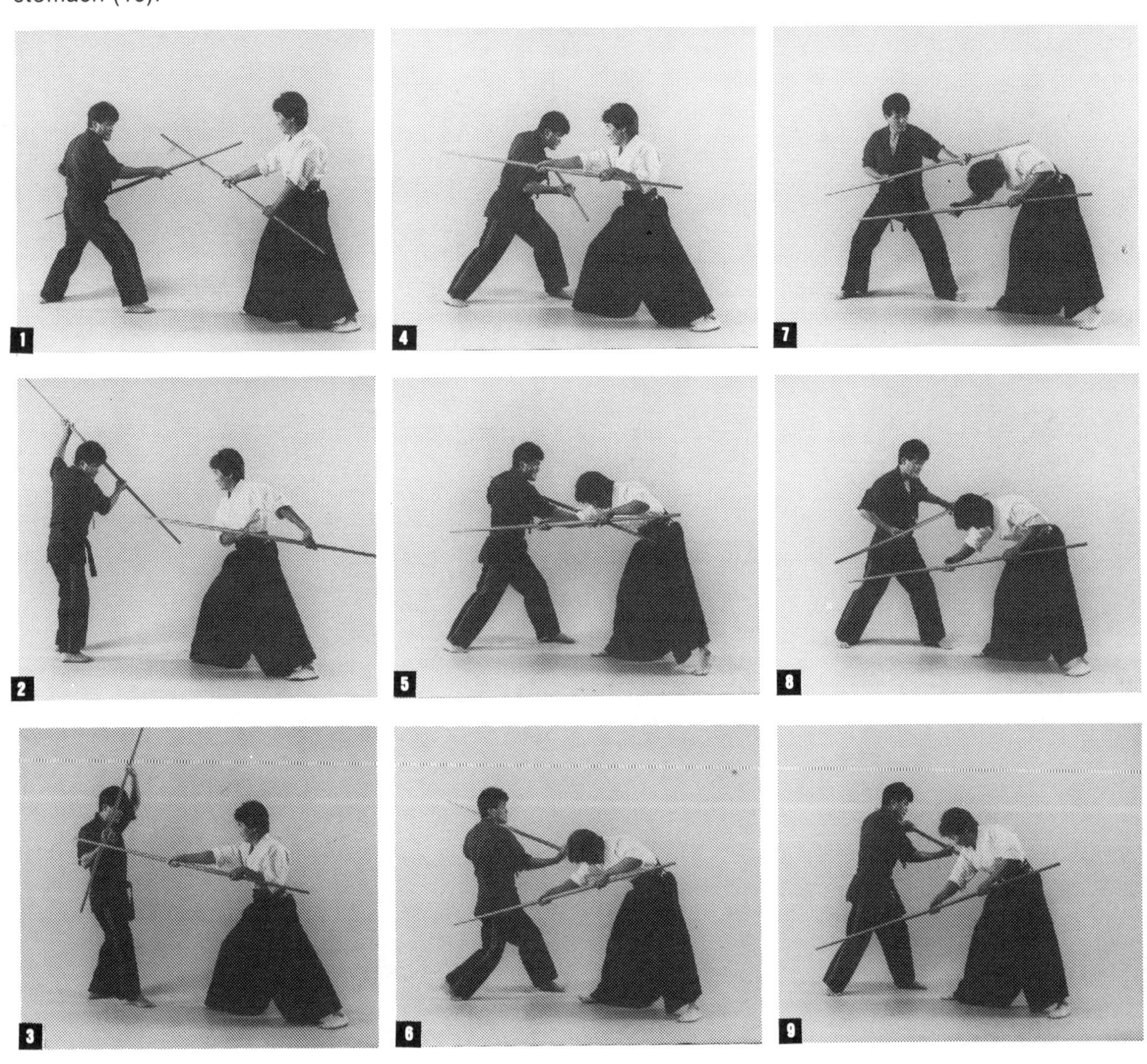

10
13
16
11
14
12
15

As the attacker sets himself (1), the defender moves into position for a side block (2). A right-hand strike is met with a block (3). The defender then grabs (4) the attacker's wrist and pulls him off balance (5). He then twists (6) the attacker and he falls (7) to the ground.

From the ready position (1), the attacker prepares (2) for a right-hand strike. But the blow is stopped with a side block (3). The defender turns 180 degrees counterclockwise (4) and twists his bo down (5). He then thrusts the tip into the attacker's stomach (6-7). Moving the attacker's bo out of the way (8), the defender prepares for the final move by sticking the bo into an unprotected arm (9). He then thrusts the bo into the attacker's stomach again (10).

7

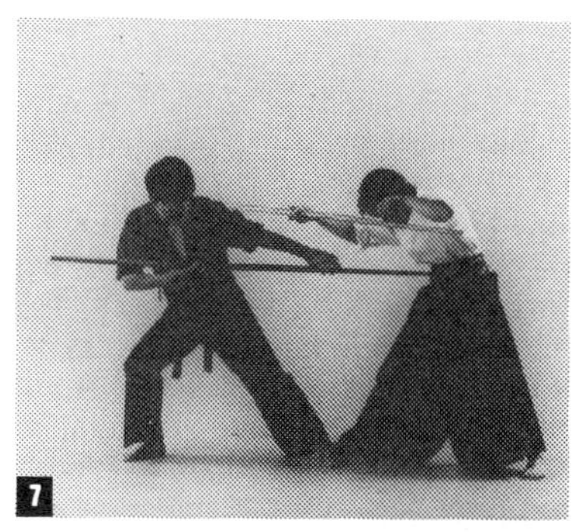

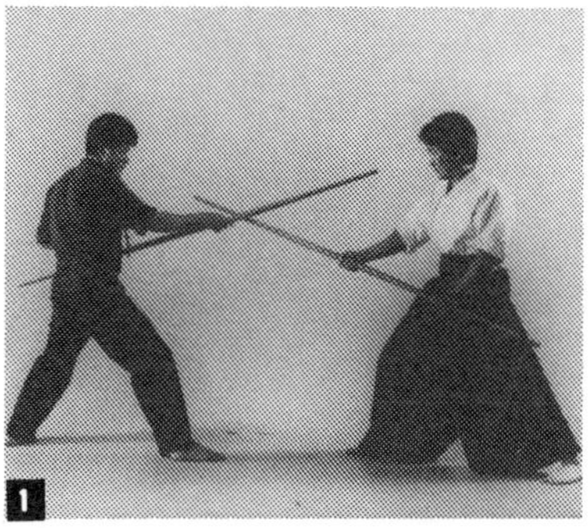

1

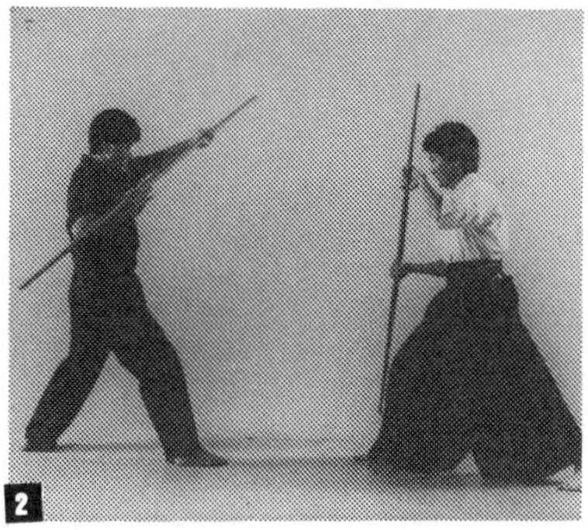

2

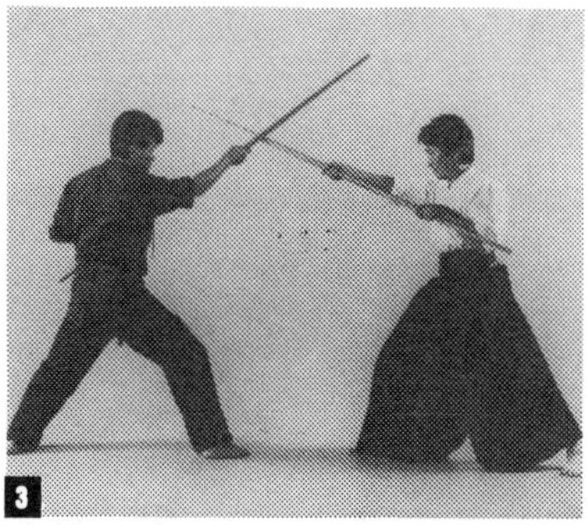

3

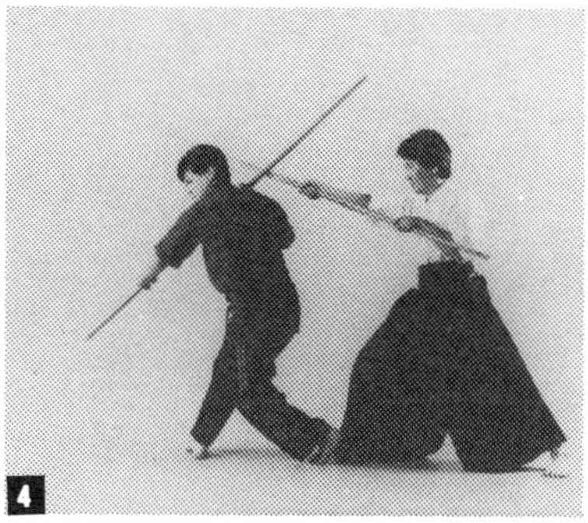

4

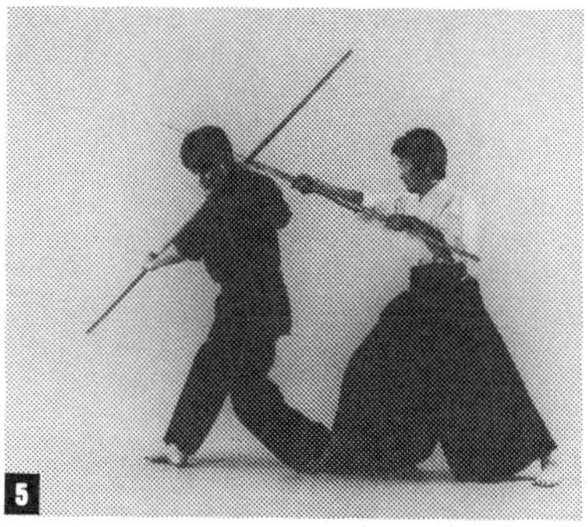

5

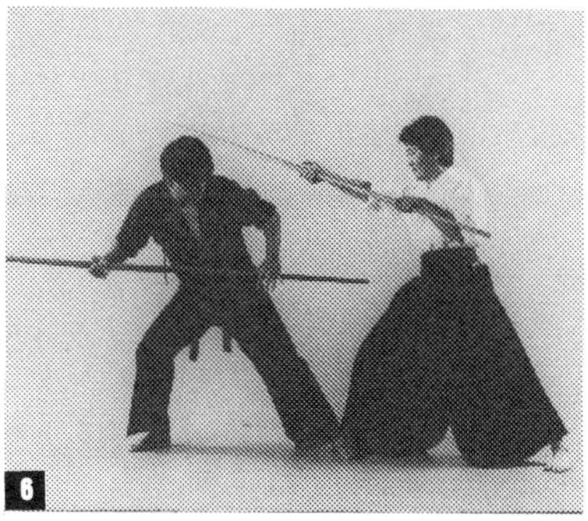

6

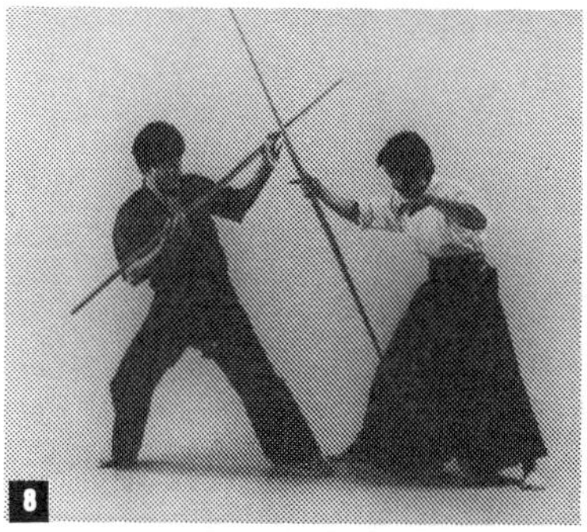

8

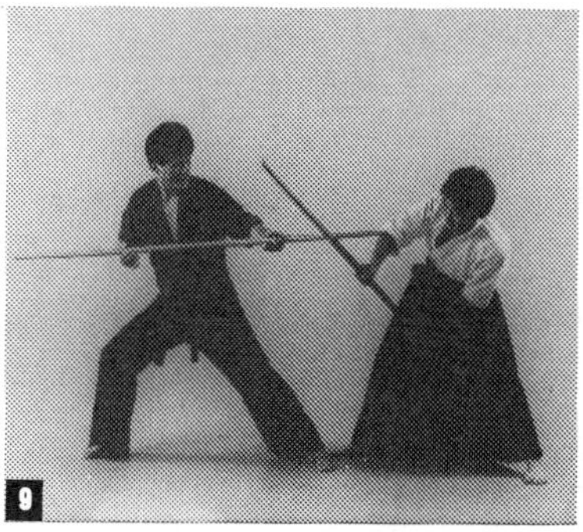

9

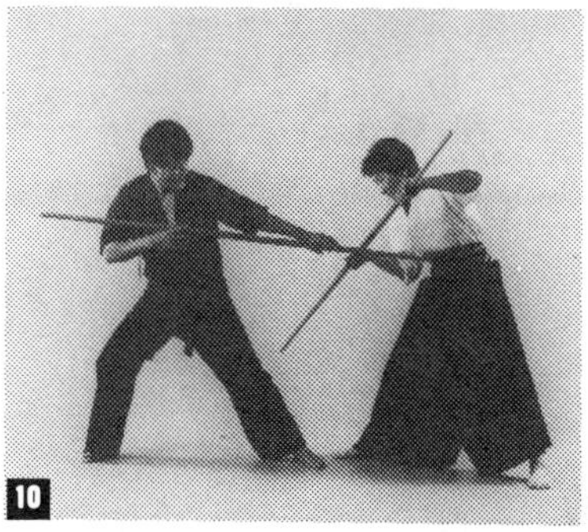

10

In this sequence (1), the attacker begins with a right-hand strike (2). The defender stops the blow with an overhead block and then pokes (3) the bo into the arm of the attacker. This causes him to drop the right-hand grip (4). The defender then raises his bo (5) and prepares for a downward strike to the head (6). He returns with a left-hand strike to the side of the head (7). Pulling the bo back (8), he slams the tip of the bo into the attacker's midsection (9).

The practitioners square off (1), and then the attacker prepares (2) for an overhead strike. The defender lifts his bo over his head (3) and blocks the strike (4). He then brings the bo down (5) to the ground (6). Bringing the bo back up, he strikes the attacker's groin (7). The attacker doubles over (8) and the defender flips him on his side (9).

In this series, the defender prepares for a right-hand strike (1-2). He stops the blow with a side block (3) and begins spinning both bo clockwise (4-6). Sensing an opening (7), he applies a right-hand strike (8) to the side of the head. A strike to the knee (9) follows. He then puts the bo between the attacker's legs (10) and lifts him off the ground (11).

You should use leverage when two people are fighting for the bo (1). Step 90 degrees to the left and raise the bo so that it is vertical (2). Twist the weapon around his neck (3) and push the tip into his groin (4). Lift up (5) and he'll fall (6).

When fighting for the bo (1), you can easily just shove one end into his stomach (2). Or if you are in another position , release your grip (3) and grab his wrist (4). Bring up the wrist (5) and twist it while pulling it down (6). As his body follows (7), it will be easy to flip him over (8).

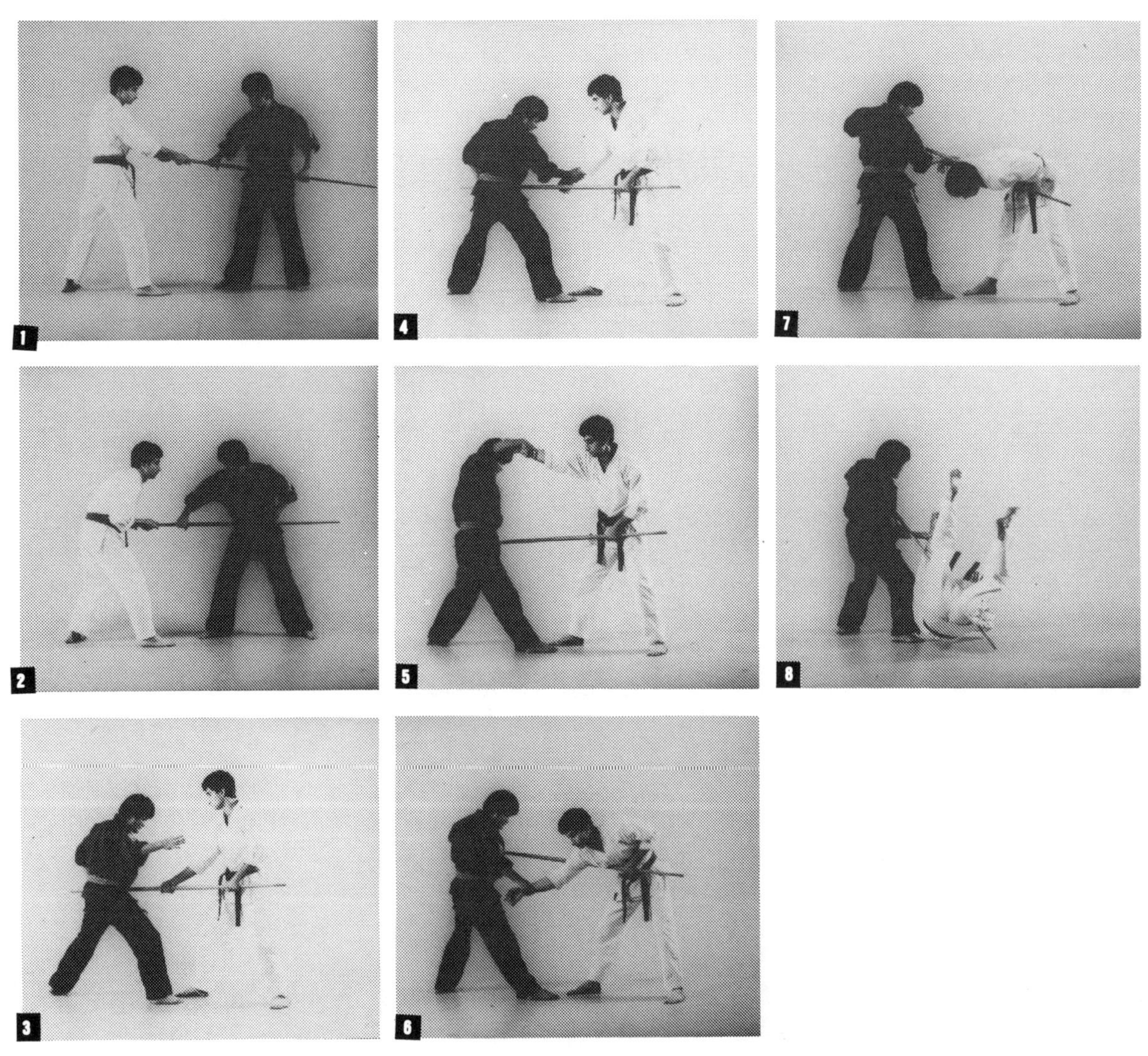

Another simple way to gain control (1) is to twist the bo (2), with the left hand coming over the top (3). With his hands tangled, he is powerless (4). Grab the bo from his grip (5), and thrust the tip into the neck (6). He will fall harmlessly to the floor (7).

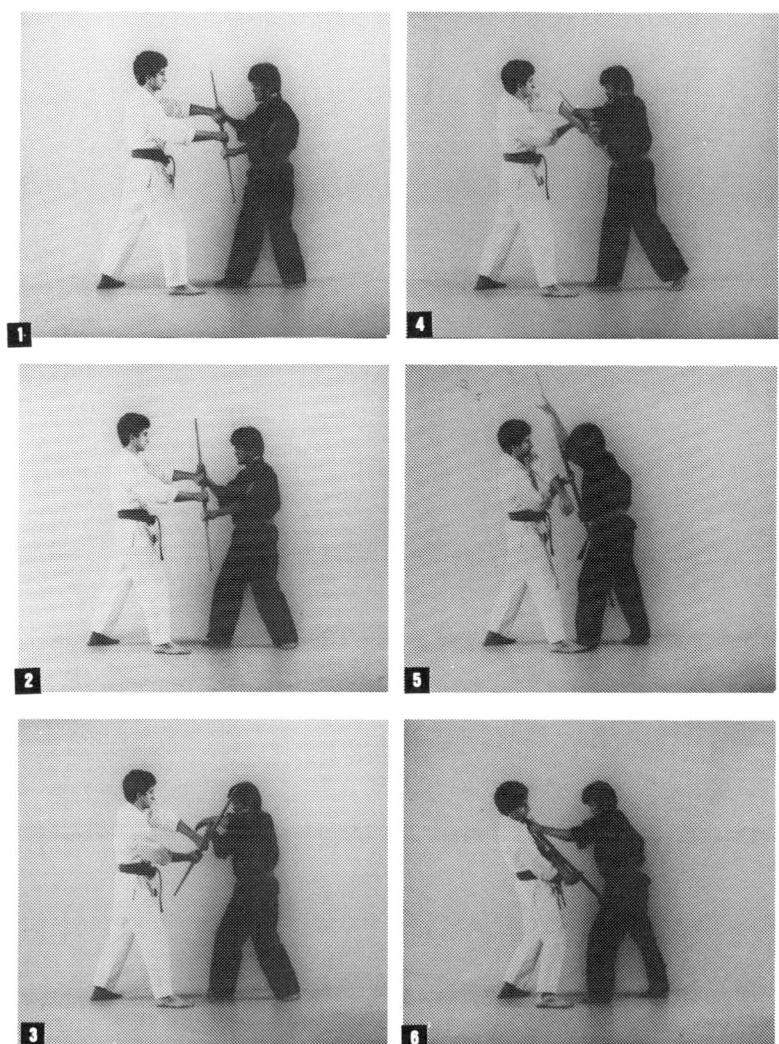

From a ready position (1), the attacker gets set to deliver a right-hand strike (2). The defender steps to the side (3) and blocks the blow. He then brings his bo over (4-6) and pushes down the attacker's weapon. A thrust to the stomach subdues the attacker (7).

Preparing to defend against a downward strike (1-2), the defender ducks under the weapon while blocking at the same time (3). He then thrusts his bo (4) against the inside of the attacker's wrist. By pulling up on his bo (5), he loosens the attacker's grip on the weapon. He then reaches down and strikes the back of the leg (6) with the lower end of the bo. As the attacker begins to fall (7), the defender thrusts the bo into his ribs (8).

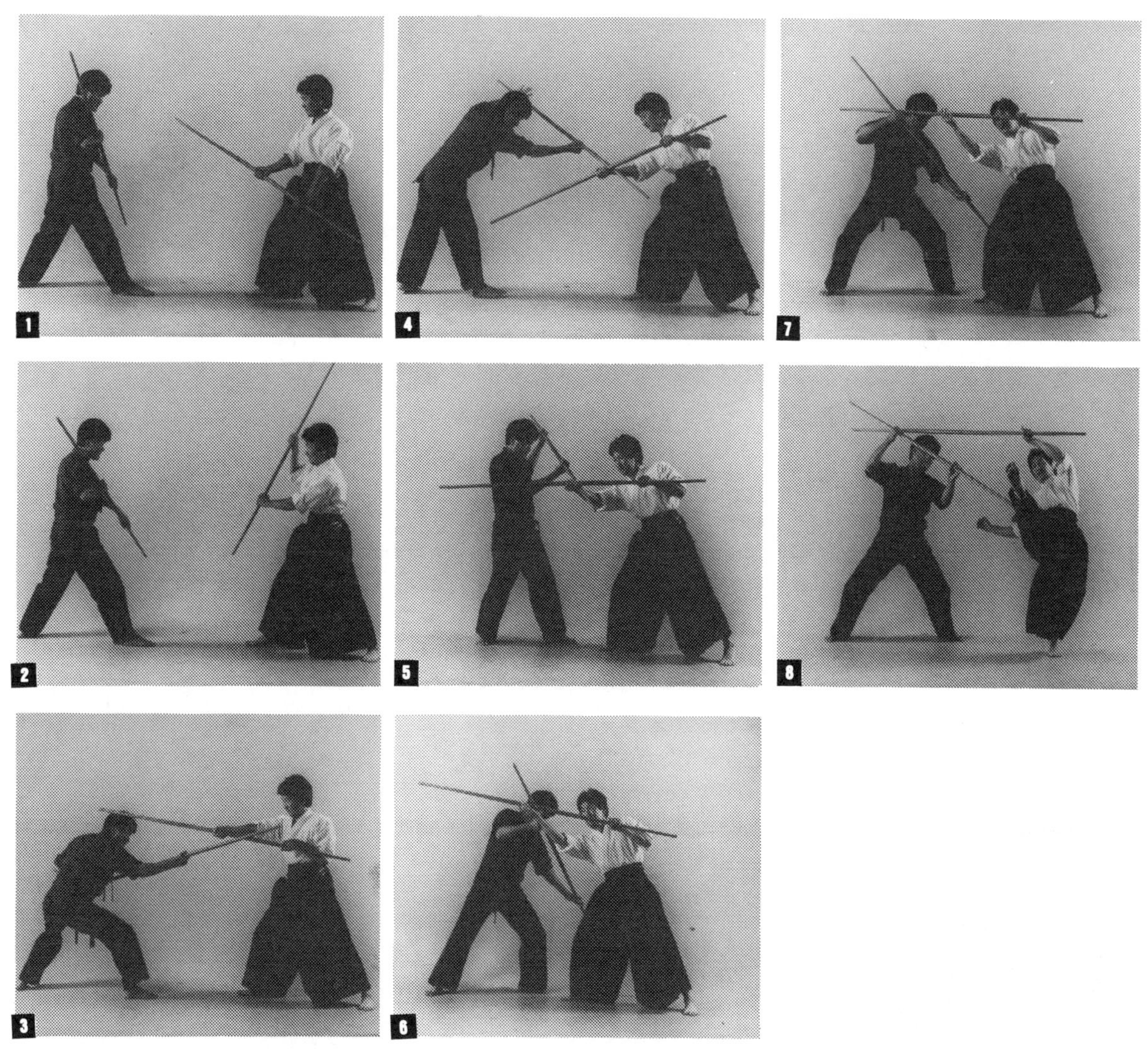

As the attacker prepares for a right-hand strike (1-2), the defender steps to the side and executes a downward block (3). He then throws his bo at the attacker (4) while grabbing the enemy's bo. He takes the attacker's bo (5) and sticks its owner in the ribs and stomach (6-7).

The defender prepares for a forward thrust (1). As the attacker pulls back the bo(2),the defender raises the weapon over his head. A downward block (3) stops the blow as he steps to the right. Pulling himself up (4), he blocks another forward thrust (5) and then raises both bo counterclockwise (6). Off balance, the attacker is ripe for a thrust to the ribs (7) or a right-hand strike to the head (8).

Preparing for a forward thrust (1), the defender turns to his right and executes a side block (2). He then throws his bo at his opponent while grabbing the enemy weapon (3). As the attacker loses his grip on the bo (4), the defender retrieves his and prepares (5) for an upper thrust. He disables his foe with an upper thrust to the neck (6).

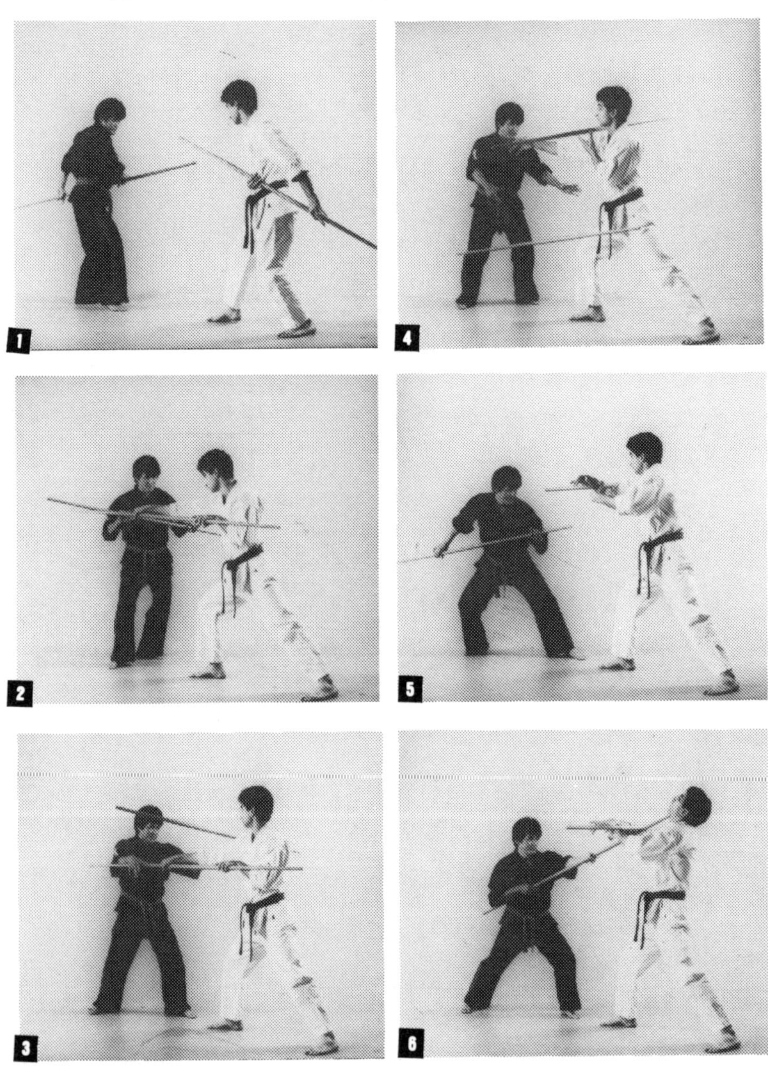

The attacker is ready to strike (1). He pulls back the bo (2) and thrusts. The defender blocks the blow (3) and then pushes (4) the weapon down clockwise. Placing his bo between the attacker's wrist and weapon gives him leverage (5). He twists over the bo (6), toppling the attacker, and finishes with a downward strike to the head (7).

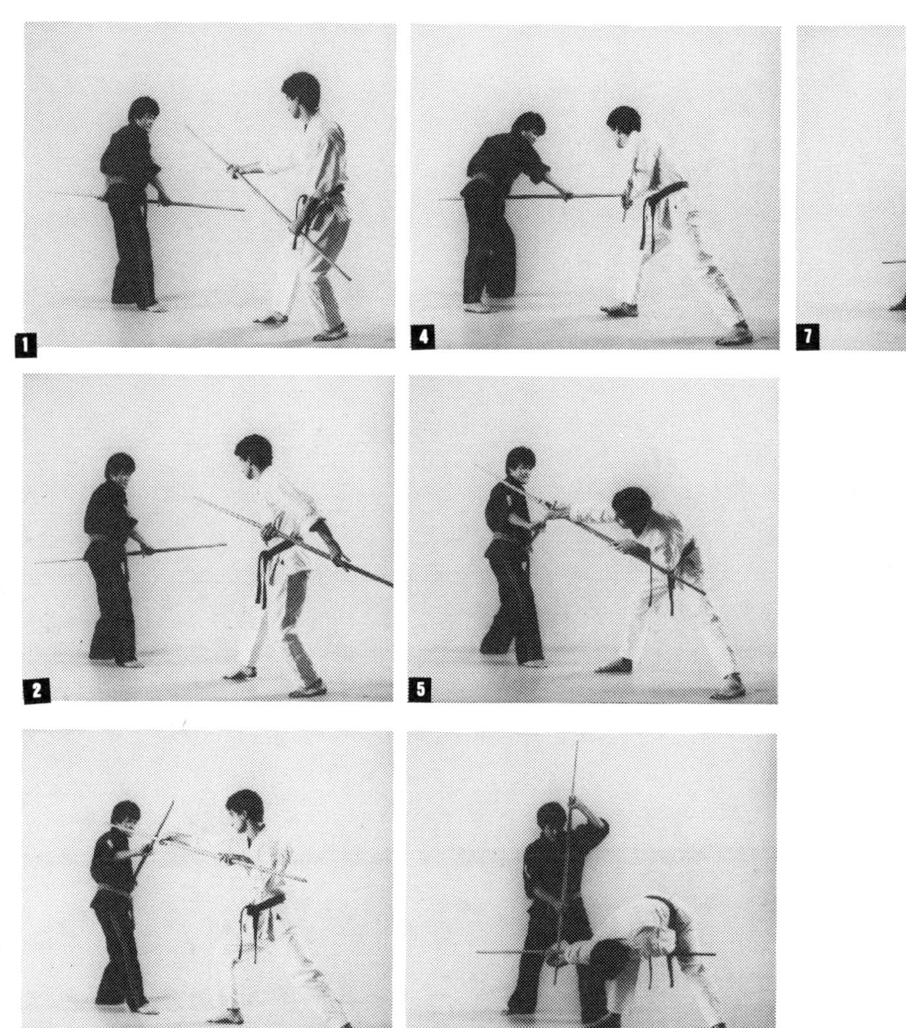

Sensing a possible forward thrust attack (1), the defender moves his bo in a vertical position(2). He then applies a vertical (3) block to the incoming thrust. He catches the thrust with his bo (4) and wedges it against his chest. By sliding his bo down and putting pressure on the attacker's weapon, he forces his attacker to lose his grip (5). Defenseless (6), the attacker is an easy target for a crosshand strike to either side of the head (7-9).

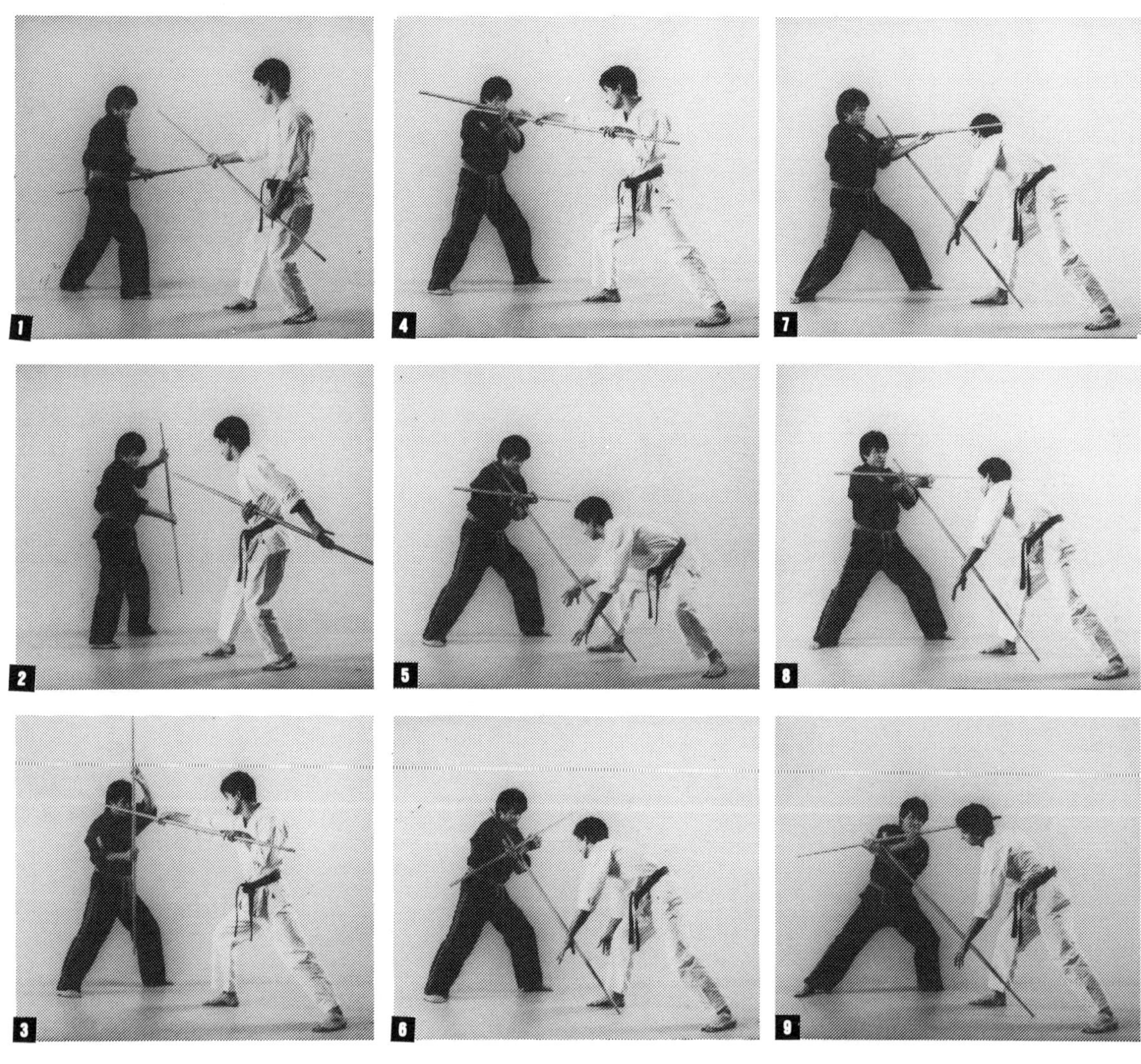

Shown here are some of the more effective bo blocking techniques (1). The attacker begins the attack (2), but the defender steps forward and blocks the blow with the upper bo tip (3). The attacker counters with a left-hand low strike (4), but the defender executes a low block (5). The defender pulls his bo back (6) and is in perfect position to block a right-hand overhead strike (7). The defender takes the offensive (8) and attempts a right-hand strike(9),which is blocked. Thwarted, both practitioners pull back their weapons (10).

7

1

4

8

2

5

9

3

6

10

The attacker prepares to strike (1). He thrusts the bo but the blow is stopped with a side block (2). The defender brings back his bo (3) and applies a left-hand strike to the side of the attacker's head (4).

From a ready position (1), the defender blocks the attacker's strike by turning to the side (2). Since the defender's bo is underneath the attacker's weapon (3), he lifts up and brings the bo over (4). He pushes his opponent's bo toward the ground (5), recoils (6), and thrusts his weapon into his enemy's neck (7).

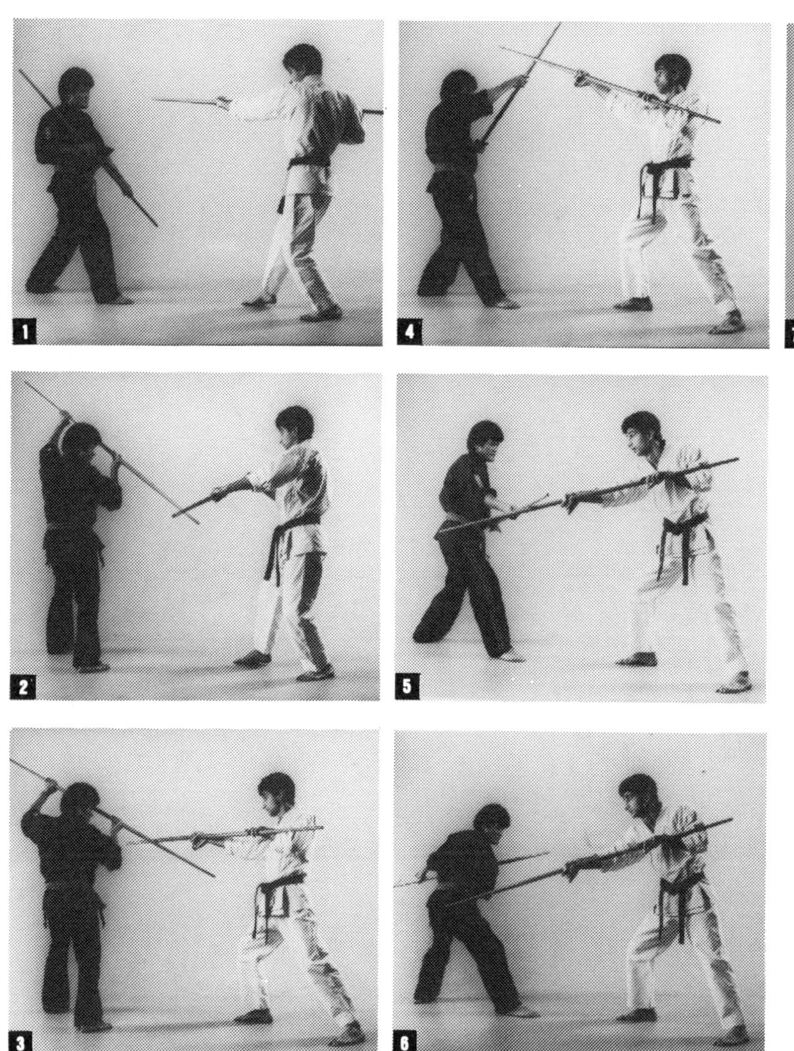

The attacker shifts his weight forward (1) and attempts a right-hand strike (2). Thwarted, he takes care of his opponent with a left-hand smash to the ribs (3).

1

2

3

As the opponent prepares to strike (1), the defender steps to the side (2) and stops the blow with a vertical block. He is now in perfect position (3) for a strike to the wrists (4) or a left-hand strike to the back of the head (5).

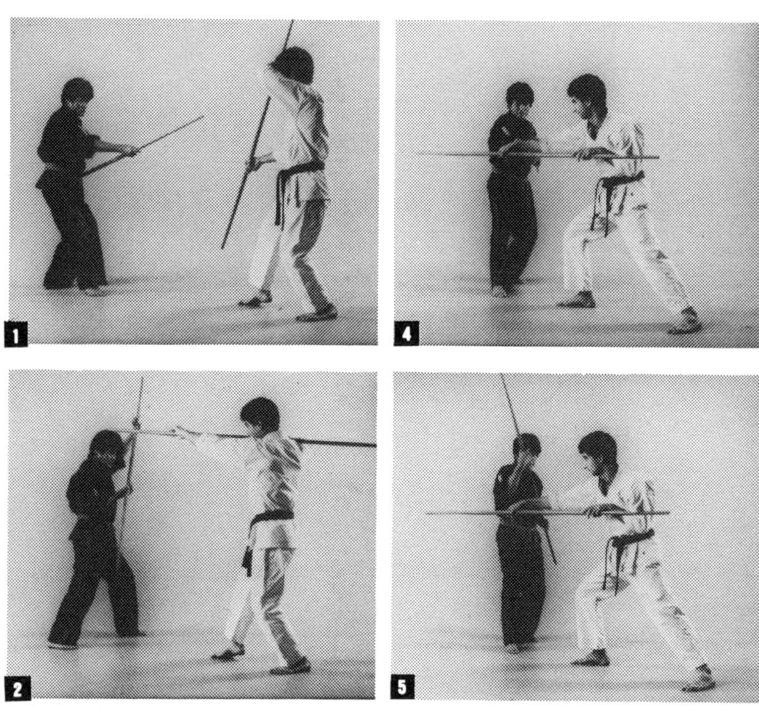

At the beginning of this sequence, the defender's right foot is forward (1). But as the attacker moves in (2) with a right-hand strike, the defender will turn to his right (3) to block the blow. He then pushes the attacker's bo down and out of the way (4). With a clear opening, he brings back his bo (5) and thrusts it into the attacker's stomach.

1

2

3

4

5

The attacker's weight is on his front foot as he prepares for a downward strike (1-2). The defender thwarts the blow with a downward block (3) and then brings the opponent's bo up with a counterclockwise swing (4). The attacker is off balance (5) and the defender can finish him off with a right-hand strike to the back of the knee (6).

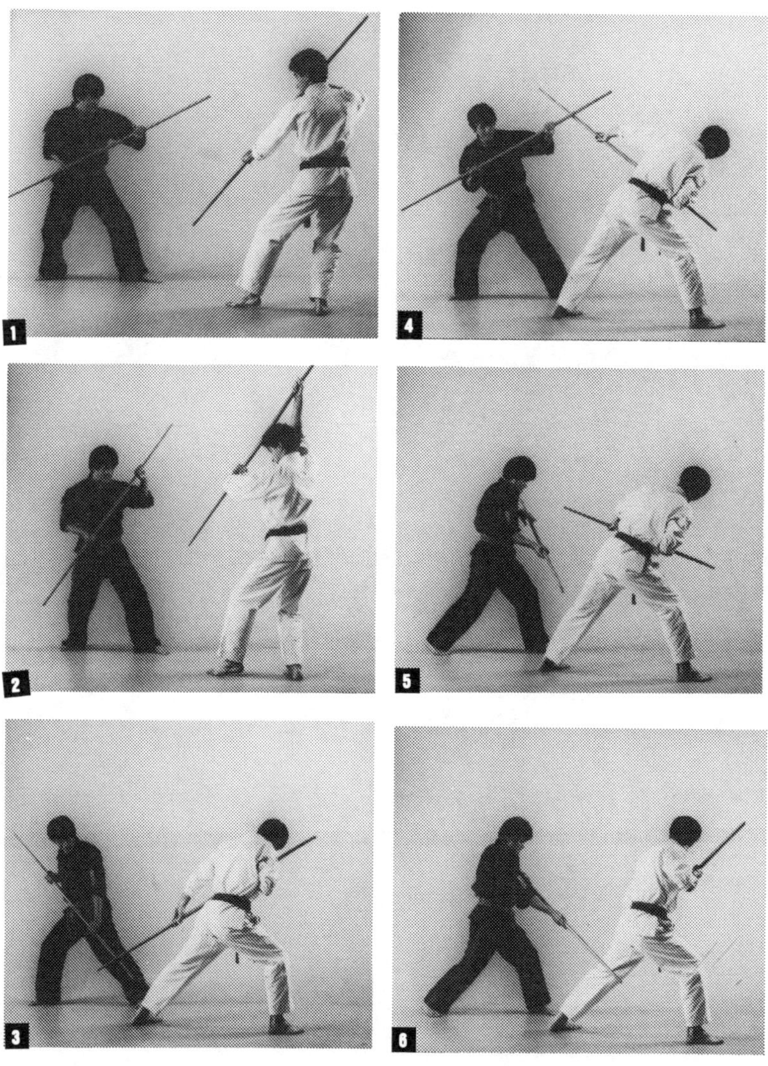

MODERN-DAY USES OF THE BO

The fighting aspect of the bo may be 500 years old, but it has never outlived its usefulness. In fact, the bo and its derivatives may be as valuable today as they were during Emperor Hashi's takeover of Okinawa in the 14th century.

Obviously, the use of the long staff in street self-defense is nearly impossible. You just cannot take a 12-foot long stick with you to the shopping mall or the movies. However, there are offshoots of the weapon which could be lifesaving in a potentially lethal situation.

Despite the bo's awkwardness on the street, the study of the weapon is very popular in dojo around the world. Japanese, Chinese and Okinawan karate teachers offer the art of bojutsu because of its historical ties with another martial arts era. It is especially imperative that boys in Okinawa learn the weapon, as well as the sai and nunchaku, because of its connection with the past.

The most popular uses of the bo today are in the areas of health and recreation. Not only is the bo an excellent way to build strength and stamina, it is one of the more favorite weapons in demonstration circles. Many people want to learn the bo for its health benefits. Thanks to its varying sizes and weights, the bo is an important exercise tool. Used much like a bar. without free weights attached, the bo can be lifted, swung or pulled.

The most practical use for learning the bo is in the application of its techniques to other common tools. In Japan, many of the older countrymen use a walking cane or umbrella when they go out after dark. By knowing the techniques of the bo, these two simple pieces of equipment are deadly effective in the event of an attack. A kendo stick or jo stick work just as well when the situation arises.

A weapon does not become a weapon until it lands in the hands of a trained user. Learning the basics of the bo can turn that umbrella or walking stick into a tool of self-defense. It worked for an oppressed people 500 years ago, and it can work for you today.

While reading this book should give a much better understanding of the bo or long staff, as well as its history, self-defense applications and modern-day uses, it cannot hope to serve as the end total of your training. Proper instruction, combined with training aids such as technical books and video tapes, will provide a well-rounded curriculum in your education of the bo.

As you begin your intensified study of the bo, it will help to remember eight points. Be careful. A weapon used right is only dangerous to an opponent. A weapon used incorrectly is only dangerous to oneself.

1. Dodge an opponent not by sheer power, but with your body. Always place yourself in the best position for a strike or block. Good positioning is one of the keys to success.

2. Continue the pursuit of long staff knowledge long after you think you've mastered the weapon. Don't come under the misconception that there is nothing left to learn. Masters who trained for 40 years also trained an extra day.

3. Karate and *Ryu Kyu* martial arts were originally very similar. In fact, the movements of karate lay the foundation for bo techniques. Only by learning karate can a practitioner hope to master the long staff.

4. Study the spirit that comprises real zanshin.

5. You must be able to use your weapons but never totally depend on them. The study of the martial arts teaches us first and foremost the need for self-discipline and self-control. Only when all avenues have failed should we reach for our weapon. It should be a last resort, rather than a first strike.

6. To teach bojutsu is easy. But only maximum effort and practice will help you learn it completely.

7. The technique of the bo is synthetic in nature. The technique of the sai comes from the shuto system. The technique of the tonfa is of the uraken and elbow-strike systems.

8. Nunchaku belongs to the bo class and has been called the "portable bo."

BO STRIKES

Before you can think about learning the common strikes of the bo, it is important to know how to handle this delicate weapon. Mishandling the weapon is the quickest way to an incorrect strike method.

1. Both hands on top.

2. Left hand on top, right hand underneath.

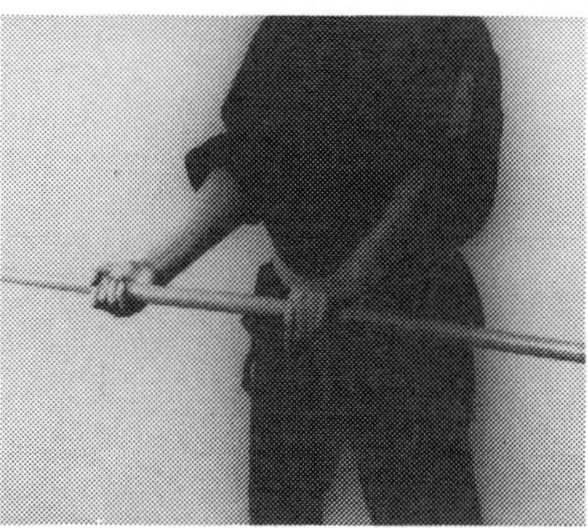

3. Right hand on top, left hand underneath.

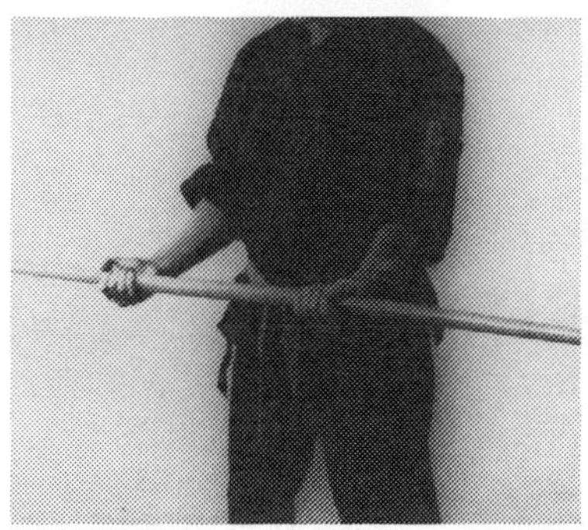

4. Both hands underneath.

The strikes come through learning the five basic bo positions:

Chudan-Kamae.

Jodan-Kamae.

Gedan-Kamae.

Waki-Kamae.

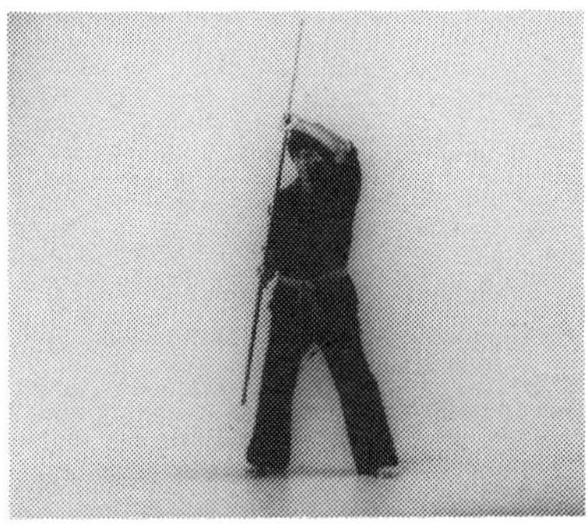

Hasso-Kamae.

Right-hand strike

From the hasso-kamae position (1), bring the bo back (2), step forward and snap with the right hand (3).

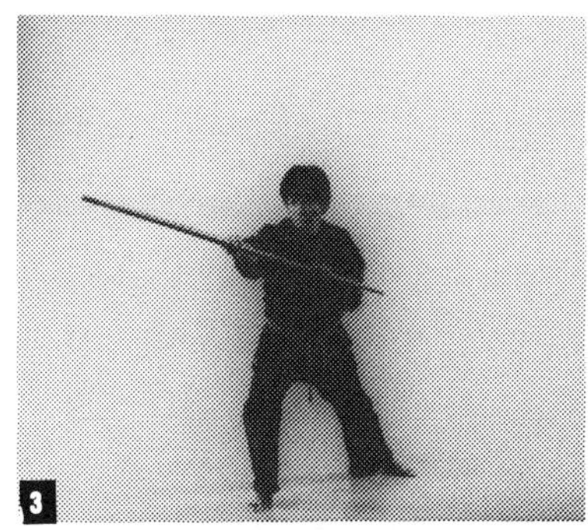

Left-hand strike

From the set position (1), step forward (2), and snap the bo with your left hand (3).

Left half-moon strike

With the bo diagonal across your face (1), swing the bo across your body with your right arm (2).

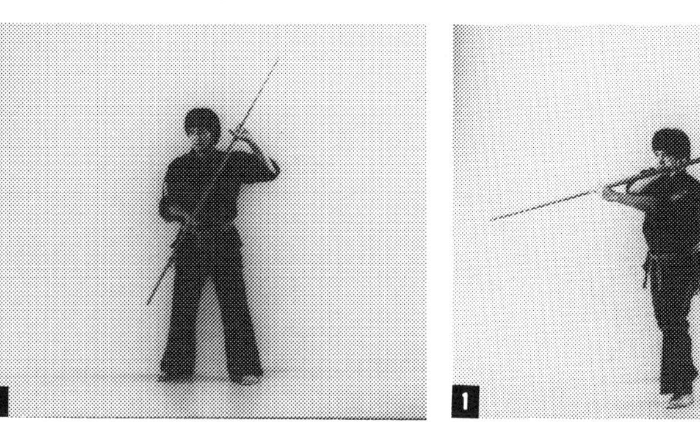

Downward thrust

From a set position with the right foot forward (1), twist the bo as you thrust forward (2). Twist again and return to your original position (3).

Low strike

From the set position (1), step forward and swing your left hand down (2).

Downward strike

Bring up the bo (1) and shove it down (2).

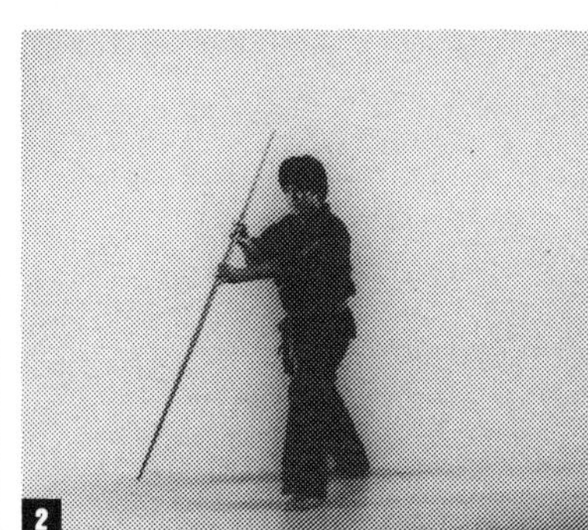

Right-hand strike

From the set position (1), bring the bo back (2), and snap it with your right hand (3).

Forward thrust

From a set position (1), bring the bo back (2) and thrust it forward, placing all your weight on your right leg (3). Bring it back (4) and thrust it forward again (5).

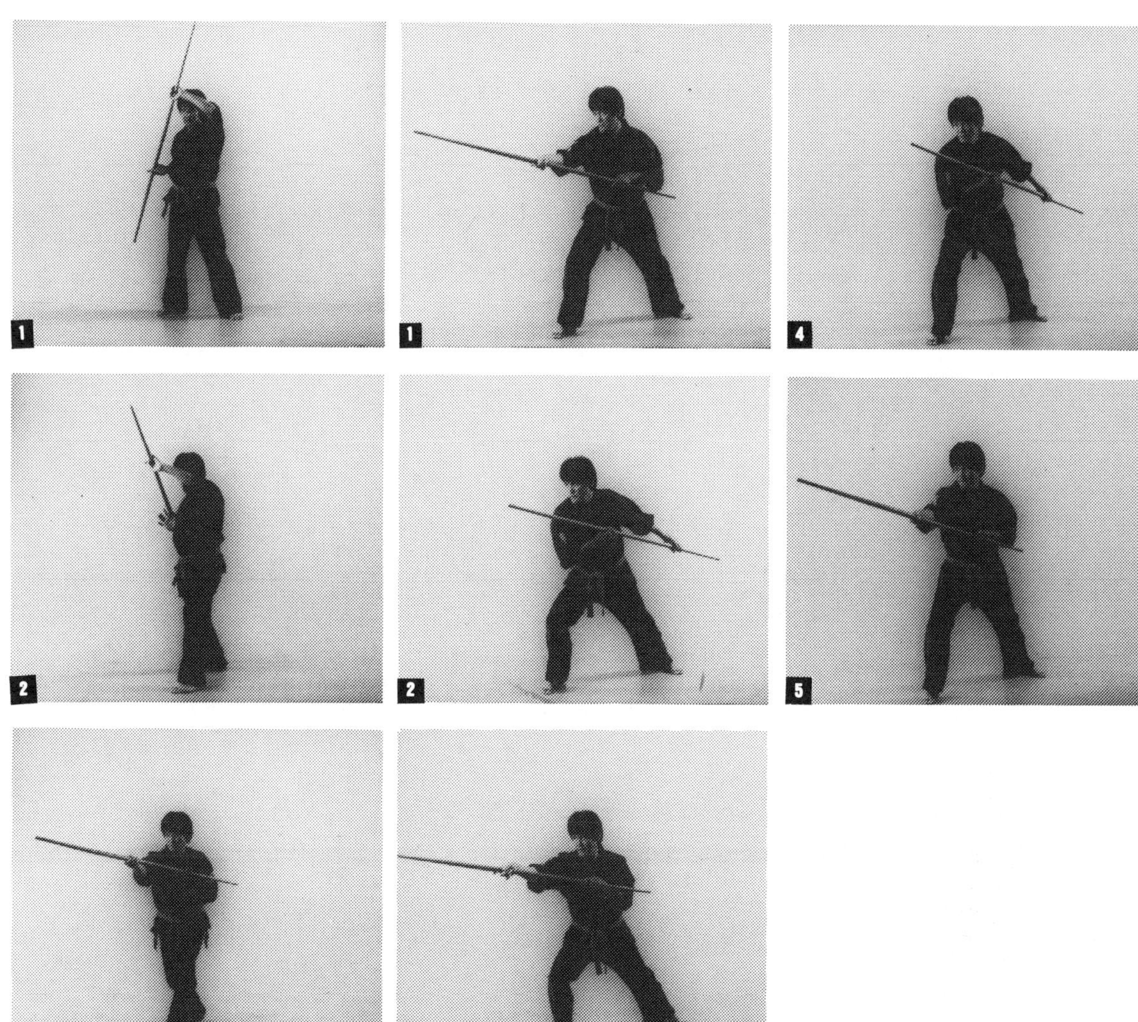

Assume a cat stance with the bo in a diagonal position (1). Pull the bo back (2) and then over your head (3). Snap your right hand and the bo will follow (4).

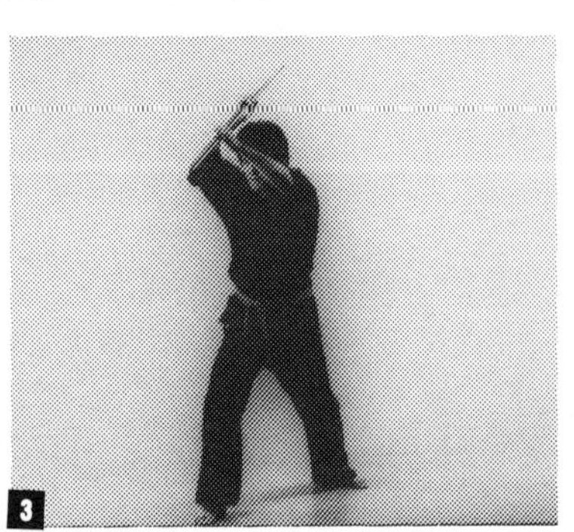

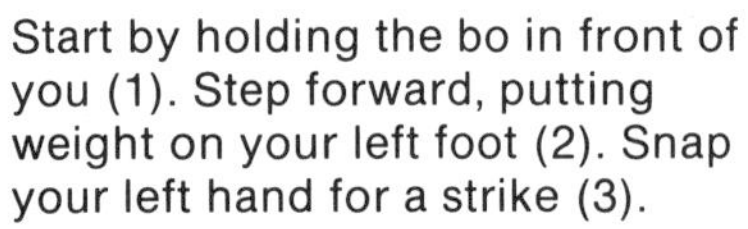
Start by holding the bo in front of you (1). Step forward, putting weight on your left foot (2). Snap your left hand for a strike (3).

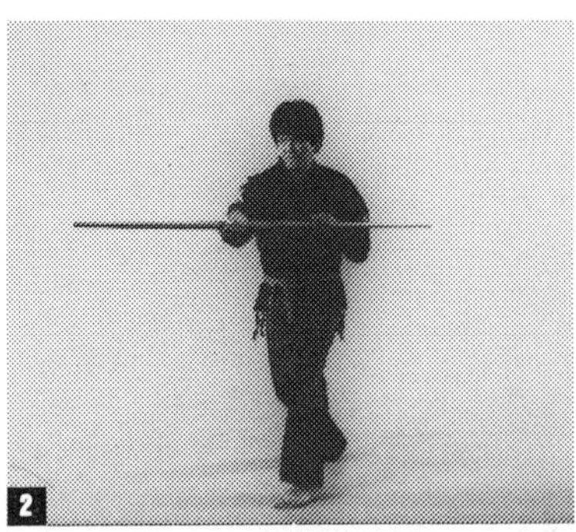

With your left foot forward and the bo at your side (1), snap your right hand (2) and then return to your original position (3).

With the bo behind your back (1), bring the bo over your head (2). Widen your hand grip (3) and swing down (4).

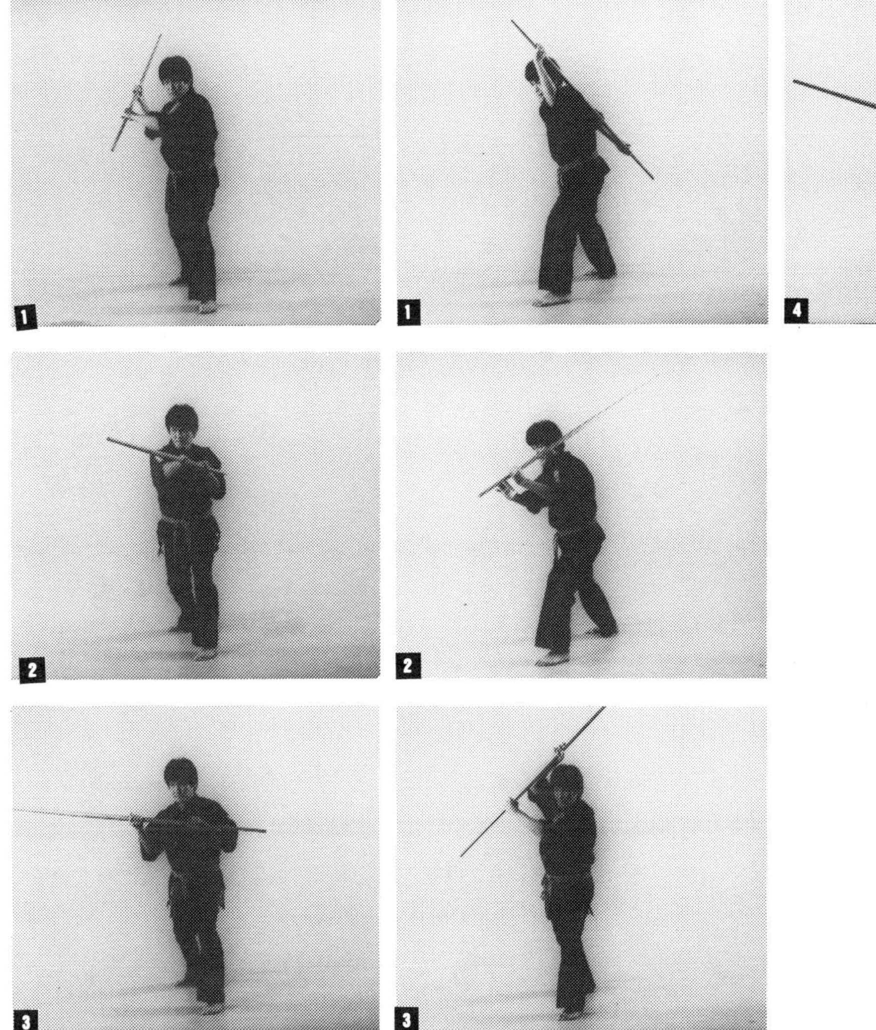

With the bo in a diagonal position in front (1), bring the bo up by turning your hand toward your head (2). Thrust the bo forward with your left hand (3).

1

2

3

From a raised position (1), swing the bo from right to left behind your shoulders (2) and then across your body with your right hand (3).

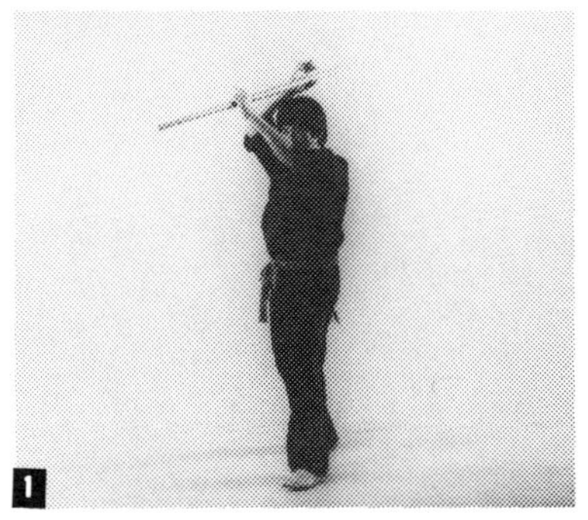

1

2

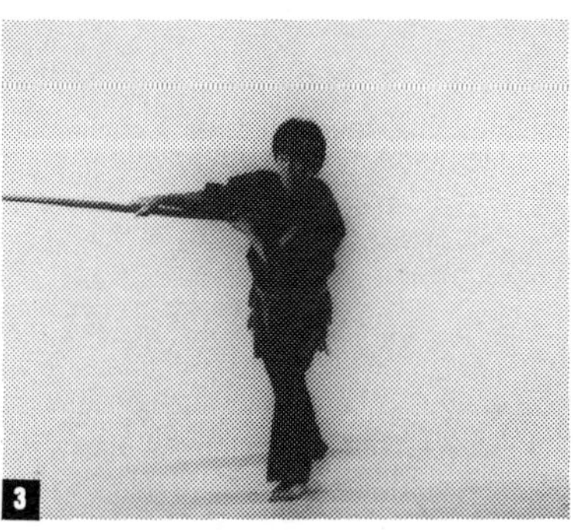

3

Shown here are low kamae positions.

Assume a cat stance and grab the bo at the end (1). Twist your wrists and pull up (2).

UNIQUE LITERARY BOOKS OF THE WORLD